D0854755

ANTHOLOGY
of AMAZING
Women

First published in Great Britain by

Twenty Watt, an imprint of Weldon Owen,
part of Kings Road Publishing,
3.08 The Plaza,
535 King's Road,
Chelsea, London,
SW10 0SZ

www.bonnierpublishing.co.uk

© 2018 Weldon Owen

Senior Editor: Fay Evans
Senior Designer: Emma Vince
Publisher: Donna Gregory

ISBN: 978-1-7834-2502-0

A CIP catalogue for this book is available from the British Library.
Printed and bound in China
2 4 6 8 10 9 7 5 3 1

ANTHOLOGY of AMAZING Women

Written by Sandra Lawrence

Illustrated by Nathan Collins

20 watt

CONTENTS

Stephanie Kwolek is an American chemist, most famous for inventing Kevlar, a synthetic material of incredible strength.

Robina Muqimyar is a former Olympic athlete who represented Afghanistan at the 2004 and 2008 Olympics.

Chimamamada Ngozi Adichie is a Nigerian writer who has been awarded a MacArthur Genius Grant.

INTRODUCTION

A comic once said of the famous Hollywood actress Ginger Rogers that she did everything her even-more-famous partner Fred Astaire did – only she did it "backwards and in high heels". Throughout history, as men have achieved extraordinary feats, women have been there too, often doing the same things, while dressed in long skirts, corsets, and high heels. That is, of course, if they've even been allowed to do it in the first place.

Men and society have traditionally made all kinds of excuses to explain why women "can't" do things. Sometimes they come right out and say "you're not good enough", but more often they make women feel unsure of what they are able to do by suggesting that if they want to be anything more than wives and mothers, there must be something wrong with them.

Girls have been told they're "too delicate" and that they need to be protected. They're brought up to believe that if they put themselves forwards or stand up for themselves, then people won't like them – that they're "showing off" or just plain weird. If all else fails, some men resort to the "strength" argument, saying girls are physically weaker than boys – which, while it might sometimes be true, means very little. Just ask the Women's Timber Corps of the Second World War who did forestry work in Britain while the men were away fighting. "Lumberjills" proved that the work jealously guarded by Lumberjacks was tough, but by using proper techniques it was perfectly doable by women.

The WTC (Women's Timber Corps) was disbanded in 1946, and each member was awarded a personal letter signed by Queen Elizabeth for their service.

Women who want something more in life are told they are unnatural. People say they'll let down their children, dishonour their families, and, worse, they'll be unfeminine! Society has been spinning this line for so long that many girls and boys have been persuaded to believe it. Who knows how many extraordinary, would-be achievements never happened because women were forced to stay at home, told they couldn't have a family and at the same time, make a difference to the wider world?

Many milestones have only been cleared in recent years. Women in the UK earned the right to vote in 1918, and the legal right to equal pay in 1970. Happily, throughout history, there have been the Amazing Women prepared to stand up to society, no matter the cost. Many have had to sacrifice a "normal life" – friends, families, love, children, and occasionally, even, their lives – but they're just not prepared to sit by and watch others do something that they could do better. It is important for us to remember that though these problems have existed throughout history, change is possible, and things will continue to get better.

"Rosies" (named for the iconic "Rosie the Riveter") were the women who worked in munitions factories and shipyards during The Second World War.

There are eight sections in this book: Art and Design, History, Politics, Science, Sports, Music, Film and TV, Literature, and Business, but there are amazing women in pretty much every aspect of life. Everyone mentioned here is extraordinary, but they are only the tip of an incredible iceberg. It was very hard to choose who to include – a separate book on each subject could exist, and there still would not be enough room for the thousands of brilliant women who need to be celebrated. For now, though, here are some of my favourites. Perhaps after reading them, you'll be inspired to come up with a list of your own. Better still, maybe you'll become an amazing woman or man yourself!

Sandra Lawrence

women in...

ART & DESIGN

Who knows who made the first paintings? People always assume it was cave "men" but we just don't know, and several of those prehistoric handprints on cavern walls are female.

All through the ages women have made art, even when they weren't supposed to, and sometimes when they were not even allowed to. Today, there are thousands of female artists. Their gender doesn't matter; all anyone cares about is how good the art is. Thanks to the pioneering women who opted to stand out from the crowd, everyone can make an artistic expression in every area of art and design.

MARY COLTER
USA

Mary was one of the very few female architects in the early twentieth century. Inspired by Native American art, she designed a series of innovative hotels and restaurants for entrepreneur Fred Harvey. Each "Harvey House" is extraordinary, different, and inspiring.

GUNNBORGA THE GOOD
Scandinavia

Gunnborga is the only recorded female "rune-master" in Viking-Age Scandinavia. Experts are not sure whether or not she actually carved the runes into the massive stone in Jättendals Church in Sweden, but the inscription clearly states that Gunnborga coloured it.

ARTEMISIA GENTILESCHI
Italy

One of the most accomplished painters of her time, Artemisia was a talented Baroque-era artist. In a time where women were not easily accepted by the artistic community or patrons, she was the first woman to become a member of the *Accademia delle Arti del Disegno*.

OEI KATSUSHIKA
Japan

Oei Katsushikia was the daughter of a famous traditional print artist called Hokusai. Her brand of woodblock printmaking broke the rules – she showed people with their backs to the viewer, and she may have been the first Japanese artist to depict a night scene.

YOKO ONO
Japan

Yoko had been a multimedia artist in her own right for years before she married John Lennon. Often ahead of her time, much of Yoko's work was – and still is – shocking, but it makes people think. She is still making headlines in her 80s.

MARY QUANT
UK

Before Mary Quant, fashion designers made dresses for older women. Mary created Mod-style clothes for young people. She opened her boutique, Bazaar, in 1955 and named the mini skirt after her favourite car.

Lee captured the horrors of the Second World War in powerful, moving photographs.

Lee began her career as a model, but she really made her name behind the camera.

VOGUE

LEE MILLER

Lee Miller may have started out as a model, but she was much happier when she was the one taking the pictures. Lee was born in Poughkeepsie, New York, in 1907. Despite having a hard life as a child, she was determined to make a success of herself. During the 1920s, she became a fashion model for *Vogue* and moved to Paris. Lee mixed with famous surrealist artists such as Man Ray and Jean Cocteau and apprenticed with Man Ray while creating her own exciting work as a photographer. She even discovered "solarization", a photography technique that reverses black and white on an image to give a silvery glow.

Back in New York, Lee set up a portrait studio that attracted rich and famous clients, but she wanted to travel the world. She moved to Cairo, where she took photos of desert villages and ruins before moving once again, this time to London as a fashion correspondent for *Vogue* magazine.

The Second World War broke out in 1939. The US Embassy told Americans to return to the United States, but Lee decided to stay. At first her shots of London in the Blitz had a touch of her old, playful surrealism, but war was serious and Lee found a mission. She needed to see life on the front line for herself and she needed to tell the world about it.

Lee Miller, war photographer, followed US troops on D-Day, saw the joyous Liberation of Paris, witnessed fighting in Luxembourg and Alsace, the terrible burning of St. Malo, and perhaps most distressing of all, the liberation of Nazi concentration camps at Buchenwald and Dachau. Wherever she went, her intelligent, inquiring images exposed the horrors of war in ways words could not.

In Munich, she was allowed to photograph Adolf Hitler's abandoned house. Perhaps no other reporter could have gotten away with what Lee Miller did next: she photographed herself having a bath in the dictator's tub.

After the war, she moved back to Britain and returned to photographing fashion and celebrities. She had a child and settled on a farm in Sussex, where she reinvented herself yet again as a surrealist gourmet cook. Sometimes she would "swap" with her fellow artists, even during her time as a chef. She and painter Pablo Picasso modelled for each other. She died in 1977 at Chiddingly in East Sussex, England. Her photographs remain beautiful, haunting, and shocking today.

GEORGIA O'KEEFFE

Georgia O'Keeffe proved that art doesn't have to be "photographic" to be real. Her bold, vibrant painting inspired a whole generation of Modernist artists. Born in 1887, Georgia grew up on a farm in Wisconsin. Between 1905 and 1909, she studied traditional painting in Chicago and New York, learning Realist techniques. Eventually, she had to start working as an illustrator to make money.

In 1912, she became an art teacher, and while attending a summer school, she was taught by Arthur Wesley Dow, who was interested in newer, modern styles. Georgia realized that she didn't have to go down the same "Realist" route as everyone else, and she started experimenting with abstract designs. In 1916, a friend showed some of her sketches to an art dealer and photographer called Alfred Stieglitz. He was so impressed that he mounted an exhibition of her work – without asking Georgia first. She marched into his New York gallery and demanded he take the pictures down. They finally came to an arrangement and the exhibition went ahead. The two would eventually fall in love and get married.

Soon, Georgia's paintings of skyscrapers were the last word in chic in 1920s New York. She also made gigantic pictures of flowers, so close-up that they looked almost abstract. They were simple and elegant and made the viewer think differently about the subject. Always looking for a new style, she took a trip to New Mexico in 1929 where the stark, sun-parched landscape, strange rock formations, and dramatic skies suited her perfectly. She was particularly moved by the abandoned bones and skulls of animals, left to bleach in the sun, which she painted alongside flowers and against flat colours or New Mexican backdrops.

After Alfred died, Georgia moved to New Mexico permanently, but she also travelled around the world, painting the landscapes she saw, including mountains in Peru and Japan. When she was 73, she started a new series around clouds and rivers, and even when she started going blind she was still bursting with creativity. At 90 she was still painting, with the help of assistants.

The "Mother of American Modernism" was awarded the Medal of Freedom in 1977 and the National Medal of Arts in 1985, a year before her death. Georgia O'Keeffe is still one of America's most important painters – her painting *Jimson Weed/White Flower No. 1*, recently became the most expensive painting by a female artist ever sold at auction. Her home in Santa Fe is now a museum, national landmark, and a call-to-arms for creative women everywhere.

Georgia is admired for the honesty and boldness found in her paintings.

Georgia changed the art world and inspired later generations with her creativity.

Frida celebrated her South American heritage by wearing traditional costumes.

Frida famously painted her own portrait many times.

FRIDA KAHLO

Frida Kahlo is one of the most recognizable artists of the twentieth century, not least because of her 143 paintings, 55 are self-portraits. "I am so often alone". she once said, "and I am the subject I know best."

Frida was born in 1907 in Coyoacán, a suburb of Mexico City. In 1925 she was nearly killed in a horrific bus crash. She suffered multiple fractures to her spine, collarbone, ribs, pelvis, and shoulder. From that day on, Frida was in constant pain and would endure over thirty operations in her short life. While in the hospital, Frida's father gave her some paints. Her mother made her a special easel so she could work lying down and rigged up a mirror so she had a subject – herself. In art, Frida found her voice, a way of expressing her psychological and physical wounds. She used symbolism to describe her distress: perhaps scissors, surrounded by her own fallen hair, or a broken heart lying at her feet. In other work she depicts herself more than once, showing different aspects of her personality. Some were shocked at the frankness with which she bared her soul; most found it exhilarating.

Oddly, during her lifetime, Frida was often talked of as the wife of the famous mural artist Diego Rivera. Today, he is remembered as Frida's husband! Their relationship was stormy and passionate. They once even divorced but remarried a year later. Everything she felt and experienced was poured into her work. The torment of her broken body after the bus crash became a painting called *The Broken Column*, referring to her own spine. Frida partly wore her colourful, embroidered Tehuana dresses to disguise her limp, but traditional atire was also a way of exploring her place in the history of South America.

Her first solo exhibition, in New York, 1938, was a huge success, and the Louvre in Paris bought one of her paintings the year after. Frida was internationally famous. She became a professor at La Esmeralda school of art but by now she was so sick she had to hold classes at home. She attended the opening of her first and only solo exhibition in Mexico in her bed.

Against the advice of her doctors, Frida, who had always been politically active, attended a demonstration, weakening her beyond repair. She died in 1954, in the house in which she had been born.

"They thought I was a surrealist but I wasn't. I never painted dreams, I painted my own reality."

YAYOI KUSAMA

Most amazing women are not conventionally "perfect". What makes them special is that they take things other people might call problems and make those things work for them. Yayoi Kusama has been very open about the challenges she has with her mental health, but she doesn't want to be "cured". She likes the way she is, and she uses the way her mind sees the world to create extraordinary art.

Yayoi was born in Nagano, Japan, in 1929. She had an unhappy childhood; her parents were very conservative and abusive. She found solace in art, making pencil sketches and paint-spot patterns with the tips of her fingers. Later, polka dots became one of Yayoi's many artistic themes.

Yayoi was taught Nihonga, a very classical style of Japanese painting, but she hated its rigid rules. She liked modern art styles such as Cubism and Surrealism, and she was a particular fan of Georgia O'Keeffe. She wrote to the artist, and Georgia's friendly reply gave Yayoi the confidence to leave home and move to the United States. She arrived in 1957, but her money soon ran out. She had to sleep on an old door she found in the street and dig through a rubbish bin to find food. She couldn't afford to heat her apartment, so she spent all night painting to keep warm.

Yayoi made all kinds of art, including lace-like paintings she called "Infinity Nets". She sold them for whatever she could get. Fifty years later, in 2008, one sold for US $5.1 million, then a record for a living female artist.

As she became more confident, Yayoi began to experiment, though she still felt like an outsider. She made large paintings, soft sculptures and performance art events called "happenings". She played with different media, from body painting to film and often used repeat patterns and mirrors. She explored different ways of expressing herself, writing books and holding solo exhibitions in France, New York, and England. In 1966, at the famous Venice Biennale, to which she wasn't officially invited, Yoyai produced a dazzling room full of small silver spheres, which she sold for $2 each. People who bought them would see themselves reflected in them. She called it *Narcissus Garden*. Officials stopped her "peddling" the spheres, saying it was cheapening art, but Yayoi was making a point about the sale of art and the people who buy it.

She returned to Japan in 1973 and did not stop working. She did, however, choose to check herself into in a psychiatric institution in 1977, and still lives there today, aged 89.

Yayoi holds the record for the best-selling artwork by any living artist.

Yayoi's unique way of seeing the world helps her to create art.

17

Edmonia's sculptures reflect her own ancestry and are now considered important artworks.

Edmonia dealt with brutal racism and rejection but she kept her nerve.

EDMONIA LEWIS

Female sculptors in the nineteenth century were highly unusual, but when Edmonia Lewis started, no woman of African-American origin had ever done it before. Slavery was legal in the United States until 1865, and racism was rife.

Edmonia's birth-name was Wildfire. She was born in Greenbush, New York, around 1844 to a Native American mother and Afro-Haitian father. Sadly, she and her brother Sunrise were orphaned and brought up by her mother's Chippewa community. At the age of twelve, Sunrise renamed himself Samuel and moved to California to follow the Gold Rush. He was soon able to pay for his sister to go to school, then to college in Ohio. Wildfire changed her name to Mary Edmonia Lewis, and things went well at first.

After some trouble at college, Samuel helped her move to Boston, where she was rejected by tutors because of her gender and colour. Edmonia finally met sculptor Edward Brackett who gave her a few lessons. She was a natural. With hardly any training or experience, she started creating medallions and busts of famous abolitionists and managed to sell enough to finance a trip to Europe in 1865.

Edmonia visited London, Paris, and Florence, but fell in love with Rome. The Italian language came easily to her and she opened a small studio. There were a lot of sculptors in Rome at the time because of the ready supply of marble. Traditionally, labourers would finish sculptors' works off for them, but Edmonia didn't want assistants. She wanted to keep her work as her own so no one could accuse her of not being good enough.

Although she was good at making copies of famous statues, her own work was both innovative and unique, depicting non-European subjects including black people and Native-Americans. Edmonia returned to her Native American roots with a series of sculptures based on Henry Wadsworth Longfellow's epic poem *The Song of Hiawatha*.

Edmonia went back to the United States in 1872 to attend an exhibition of her work at the San Francisco Art Association and is known to have returned a few times. She later travelled around Europe and died in Hammersmith, London, in 1907.

Few of Edmonia Lewis's works survive, but in 1991 her sculpture *The Marriage of Hiawatha and Minnehaha* were rediscovered. *The Marriage of Hiawatha* now takes pride of place at the Kalamazoo Institute of Arts.

HISTORY

In the past, most women were considered men's "property", in the care of their fathers, husbands, or brothers. Thanks to some brave women who rebelled against the system, many old, discriminatory laws are now gone, though there are still a few places in the world where that way of life remains.

These incredible women were not going to stay home – not while there were things to do, lives to save, and records to break! Men climbed mountains and hacked through jungles in stout breeches and boots, while old photographs show Victorian women doing exactly the same thing in corsets and long skirts!

AMELIA EARHART
USA

Amelia was the first female aviator to fly solo across the Atlantic Ocean. She set many other records during her lifetime, and was famously declared, "dead in absentia" after disappearing over the Pacific Ocean during her attempt at a circumnavigational flight around the world.

DOROTHY LAWRENCE
UK

On the outbreak of the First World War, budding journalist Dorothy Lawrence wanted to become a war correspondent. None of the British papers would let her go, so she disguised herself as a man and joined the British army under the name of Denis Smith.

ANNE FRANK
Germany

When young Anne Frank was forced to go into hiding with her family in Amsterdam in 1942, she kept a diary of her world. She was eventually discovered and murdered by the Nazis, but her journal has inspired millions of people in distressing circumstances.

BOUDICCA
UK

When the occupying Romans flogged her and assaulted her daughters, Boudicca, Queen of the Iceni, raised an army, destroyed Colchester, burnt London to the ground, and then did the same to St Albans. Rather than be captured by the hated Romans, Boudicca took her own life.

SACAGAWEA
USA

In 1804, explorers Lewis and Clark set out to explore Western America. Their guide, Sacagawea, gave birth on the journey, then carried her son on her back, all the while retrieving cargo from a capsized boat, finding edible plants and acting as a negotiator with people they met along the way.

LILIAN BLAND
Northern Ireland

Trouser-wearing, jiu-jitsu-practising Lillian wanted to ride in a biplane. The male aviators refused, so in 1910, Lilian built her own, using bamboo and a pair of old bicycle handlebars. Her fuel tank was a whiskey bottle and her aunt's ear trumpet!

Nellie was a brave undercover journalist, whose exposés led to positive changes.

Nellie was America's first female war correspondent during the First World War.

NELLIE BLY

Sometimes the only way to find out what's really happening somewhere is to go undercover and live with the people there. Nellie Bly, the pen name of Elizabeth Cochran, put herself in personal danger to expose cruelty, mistreatment, and injustice. Oh, and she travelled around the world in less than 80 days...

In the early 1880s, Elizabeth read an article in a Pittsburgh newspaper that said women should stay in the home, raising children, cooking, and cleaning. She was outraged and wrote a furious reply. The editor was impressed with her audacity and offered her a job at the paper. Writing as Nellie Bly, she became an undercover reporter, posing as a sweatshop worker to expose terrible working conditions, writing about unfair divorce laws, and she even went to Mexico to write about political corruption. The public was intrigued, but not everyone was impressed. Some called it "stunt reporting". Today we call it investigative journalism. Advertisers started getting uneasy, and Nellie was moved to the women's page.

In 1887, frustrated with writing about "flower shows and fashion", she moved to New York. One of her first assignments at the *New York World* was to write about a mental asylum on Blackwell's Island. She pretended to be mentally ill and had herself committed; a very dangerous thing to do. She exposed terrible cruelty, neglect, and physical abuse of patients. The state of New York was horrified and an investigation was held. New rules and regulations were introduced, improving conditions for mentally ill people. Nellie continued, going undercover in jails and factories and even looking into corruption in government.

In 1889, Nellie attempted her biggest challenge yet. As a big fan of Jules Verne's 1873 novel *Around the World in Eighty Days*, Nellie thought she could do the journey in less time than the novel's hero, Phileas Fogg. *Cosmopolitan*, a rival publication, decided to send their reporter around the world too. Elizabeth Bisland was recruited with a few hours' notice, and the world watched as the two women raced. Nellie completed the trip in 72 days, 6 hours, 11 minutes, and 14 seconds, breaking the fictional world record with a real one. Elizabeth Bisland, travelling the other way round, took four days longer but still beat Phileas Fogg!

Nellie married, and when her husband died, she took over his company, treating her workers well. The First World War broke out while she was on holiday in Europe, so she became America's first female war correspondent. Sadly, Nellie died from pneumonia in 1922 at the age of 57, but by then the style of journalism pioneered by Nellie Bly had become an industry standard.

NAKANO TAKEKO

Most people assume that samurai soldiers were all men, and in truth, most were. However, Japan has an honoured tradition of a handful of female warriors, called onna-bugeisha. They learned to fight with swords, short daggers, and a deadly, long-handled blade called a naginata. The naginata is good for women because it allows them to fight on equal terms with taller, bigger opponents. If their castle was overrun, onna-bugeisha were expected to fight to the death and die with honour. From the Empress Jing, who conquered Korea in the third century CE, to the semi-legendary Tomoe Gozen in medieval times, Japan's female samurai were not to be trifled with.

During the nineteenth century, Japan was ruled by Shoguns, a military dictatorship, but they were under constant threat from the Meiji imperial family who were fed up with just being puppet rulers. Nakano Takeko was born in 1847 in Edo, which we now call Tokyo. She learned martial arts, literature, and mathematics and became a martial arts instructor.

In 1868 the Boshin War broke out. Nakano was on the side of the Aizu clan when the Meiji imperial forces besieged Aizu-Wakamatsu Castle. The castle's women helped the wounded, made bullets and poured water over unexploded cannon balls, but Takeko wanted to fight. She wasn't allowed to join the army, so she led a troop of all-female onna-bugeisha, with her sister, Yūko, by her side. It would later be called the *Jōshitai, or* Women's Army. They wore tasuki haori (jackets) and hakama (trousers) with their hair tied back in a hachimaki (headbands). They had long and short swords tucked in their belts and carried deadly naginata in their hands.

Their opponents had repeater rifles. Twenty thousand men surrounded the castle. Takeko had just twenty women warriors, but she led the charge anyway. She cut down several enemy soldiers before she was shot in the chest.

Takeko was dying, but there was no way she was going to be taken prisoner. She knew that if her troops tried to save her she would be a drain on resources, so she asked Yūko to cut off her head and hide it so it could not be used as a trophy.

Yūko did as she was asked and buried her sister's head under a pine tree. Today, a monument next to Hōkai-ji Temple honours one of Japan's greatest samurai. In 1868, the Meiji emperor returned to power, and the age of the samurai was over. During the annual Aizu Autumn Festival, young Japanese women parade through the streets wearing hakama and white hachimaki to celebrate one of the most famous female warriors of all time.

Nakano couldn't join the men's army, so she led one for women.

Nakano was a brave, fearsome warrior, who is still celebrated in Japan.

25

Jeanne dressed as a boy so she could travel the world for her work.

Jeanne is thought to have conducted most of the important fieldwork herself.

JEANNE BARET

Sometimes we are so keen to do one amazing thing that we do another by accident. Plant fanatic Jeanne Baret just wanted to discover new specimens, but, in pursuing her quest, she became the first woman to journey around the world. She also helped classify hundreds of new species, making a serious contribution to science.

Jeanne was born in 1740 in the Loire Valley, France. Her family was very poor, and Jeanne was taught about herbs so she could practise medicine as a herb woman. In the 1760s, she met a young nobleman, Philibert Commerson, who was a botanist. He hired her to teach him about herbs, and she would later become his work partner.

In 1766, Philibert was invited to join a team of experts on a voyage around the world, but Jeanne couldn't join him because it was illegal for a woman to travel on French naval vessels. The couple came up with a cunning plan – Jeanne would dress up as a boy, call herself "Jean", and "just happen to arrive" at the ship before it set sail. Philibert would hire "the boy" as his assistant. The scheme worked. Jeanne came on board, wearing loose clothes with bandages wrapped tightly around her chest, and talking in a very deep voice. She did all the heavy work, as a boy would be expected to, and she did most of the exploring on land because Philibert had painful leg ulcers.

We don't know exactly who collected which of the more than 6,000 plant samples the two botanists amassed, but because of Philibert's health problem, it's likely Jeanne did most of it, including a particularly colourful flower from Brazil which they named Bougainvillea after the ship's commander, Louis Antoine de Bougainville.

In the spring of 1768, she was discovered, and the pair were kicked off the ship in Mauritius. The two continued their research on the island until Philibert died in 1773. Jeanne was now stuck in the middle of the Indian Ocean with no money and no friends. She married a French officer and went back with him to France where at last she was recognized, and given a pension by the government for her work. She died in 1807.

Despite her contribution to the field, Jeanne has only recently been honoured by the naming of a member of the Solanum family (which includes potatoes, tomatoes, and aubergines) after her. Its foliage is interesting, and unusual, just like Jeanne Baret.

AUD THE DEEP-MINDED

The wisdom and courage of Aud the Deep-Minded have travelled down the ages, first in tales told around firesides as early as the ninth century, then written down in the famous Icelandic sagas.

It is said that Aud was the daughter of Ketill Flatnose, a Norwegian Viking who fled Harald Finehair and sailed to Scotland. When her husband was killed, Aud and her son Thorstein the Red travelled to the Hebrides. Thorstein immediately began raiding, and eventually made a treaty with the Scots and gained half of Scotland, but he was betrayed and he, too, was killed.

Other women might have taken a new husband for protection, but not Aud. She commissioned a ship to be built in secret in the forest, loaded it with riches, then set sail in the dead of night for Iceland, the country of her brothers. She commanded a company of Vikings, servants, Celtic prisoners, and all the surviving members of her family.

After surviving a shipwreck and rejecting the help of her brother Helgi, Aud led her people to a large area called Laxdal, which she claimed before building a farm at Hvammur. She ruled as clan-chief, holding enormous feasts, settling disputes, and granting land and favours. She paid for one man's wedding and gave his wife the whole of Laxdal as a dowry. She gave lavish gifts to others, including the Celtic prisoners, who she freed.

Knowing she was growing old, Aud announced her successor at a wedding feast in order to avoid arguments. She then told her guests to drink as much ale as they liked and strode out of the mighty hall, tall and stout, as the sagas say. The party continued, but the next morning Aud was found dead in her chamber. The gathering turned into a funeral feast, celebrating the life of this extraordinary woman for many days.

On the last day, Aud's body and riches were placed into her ship, and a burial mound built over her. Usually a Viking ship funeral was reserved for great kings who had proved their worth in battle. Aud is the only recorded woman to be granted this honour.

Aud was the only woman to be granted a Viking ship funeral.

Aud the deep-minded is remembered as a strong leader of her clan.

Sojourner fought for civil rights, but she wanted gender equality too.

Sojourner made history when she successfully challenged a white man in court.

SOJOURNER TRUTH

Sojourner Truth was born into slavery. We don't know the exact date, but it's likely "Isabella Baumfree" was born around 1797 in New York. After the death of their Dutch master, her family was broken up and sold in separate lots. Nine-year-old Isabella was bundled in with a flock of sheep for $100. She was abused, beaten, whipped, and resold several times.

In 1826, slavery was about to be abolished in New York. Isabella's master said he would free her early, but he didn't and she was outraged. She later said, her head held high, that she didn't "run away", but that she walked, with her youngest daughter cradled in her arms. She had to leave her other daughter and son behind. She was taken in by an abolitionist family, but her master tracked her down and said that if she didn't come back he'd take her baby. The kindly family bought her freedom for $20. Isabella discovered that her former master had illegally sold her her five-year-old son, Peter, to a man in Alabama where slavery was still legal instead of freeing him. She sued for Peter's return, becoming the first black woman to successfully challenge a white man in a United States court.

In 1843, Isabella changed her name to Sojourner Truth when a religious experience inspired her to become a preacher. Sojourner was six feet tall and spoke with a commanding voice in a way that made people listen. She went to live with a community called the Northampton Association of Education and Industry in Massachusetts, where she met with famous abolitionists. In 1850, she published her story as *The Narrative of Sojourner Truth: A Northern Slave*. She had to dictate the memoir, as she had never been taught to read or write.

A year later she made a powerful speech at the Ohio Women's Rights Convention. She made it up as she went along, saying that black people worked as hard as white people and how, as a woman, she toiled just as hard as men. She said everyone should be treated equally. The speech became famous, under the title "Ain't I a Woman?"

During the American Civil War, Sojourner recruited troops for the Union Army and met with President Lincoln in 1864. Even for some abolitionists, her message was quite radical. She didn't just want freedom, she wanted equality, and not just for black men, but for women too. She feared that if men got civil rights, women would be forgotten. She continued to fight for women's rights, universal suffrage, and prison reform until her death in 1883. Her funeral in Battle Creek was the largest the town had ever seen.

ELIZABETH I

King Henry VIII was bitterly disappointed. He had broken from the Catholic Church in Rome and risked civil war so he could divorce his queen, who had only produced a girl. Now, in 1533, his new wife Anne Boleyn had another puny female. There went the end of the Tudor dynasty! Obviously only a boy could be a truly great monarch. But upon Henry's death in 1559, Elizabeth was crowned queen. Her brother and sister were dead; she was the only one left.

The nation was worried. They weren't to know just how clever, strong-minded, and wise this 25-year-old woman was. People advised the new queen to marry and let her husband rule. Every European prince and many English courtiers wanted to marry her. But Elizabeth wasn't having any of them. She was sharp enough to know that the problem would be with the men she didn't marry. Besides – she was yet to meet a man who would do a better job of ruling the country than she would. She stayed single, saying she was married to her country.

Elizabeth's reign was largely peaceful, a time of exploration, trade, and culture. Sir Francis Drake circumnavigated the globe. Sir Walter Raleigh founded a colony in North America, which he called Virginia, after the Virgin Queen. A bright new playwright, William Shakespeare, delighted the London theatre. Elizabeth went travelling to meet her subjects wearing expensive clothes and dazzling jewellery.

Elizabeth was especially good at juggling relations with her European neighbours. Her deft diplomacy made trade, not war, and she avoided conflict with France and Spain that other monarchs would have not been able to stop. Some wars, however, were too big even for her.

In 1588, Philip II of Spain launched a fleet of ships called the Spanish Armada, intending to invade England. Elizabeth immediately rode out to her troops at Tilbury, where, sitting on a white horse, she made her most famous speech, telling them she would fight by their side. "I know I have the body but of a weak and feeble woman", she said, "but I have the heart and stomach of a king." The Armada was defeated.

Queen Elizabeth I died in 1603, aged 69. She had reigned for 45 years. Public mourning was unprecedented and genuine. In one way Henry VIII had been right – the Elizabethan Age marked the end of the Tudor dynasty, but in everything else he was wrong. His unwanted daughter proved to be one of the greatest monarchs England has ever known.

Elizabeth gave a famous speech to her troops before defeating the Spanish Armada.

Elizabeth was smart, brave, and didn't need a man's help to rule.

With strong female advisors, Ana developed a trading nation that demanded respect.

Ana Nzingha was a fearsome king who protected her people from slavery.

ANA NZINGHA

During the sixteenth century, Portuguese slave traders, feeling the pinch from English and French rivals, looked for new territory further along the African coast. Knowing their spears were useless against the aggressors' firearms, some nations made deals, sending a few of their people into slavery to save the rest; others captured members of rival tribes to save their own. But Nzingha had no intention of giving the slave traders anything at all.

Nzingha was born around 1582, the daughter of Ngola, head of the Ndongo kingdom, in modern-day Angola. She and her brother Mbandi were trained in hunting, archery, diplomacy, and trade. Nzingha excelled, even learning Portuguese from a priest her father had captured. Ngola started a campaign against the Portuguese colonialists, and when he died, Mbandi became king.

The Portuguese suggested a treaty with Mbandi, and Nzingha was sent to conduct negotiations. She was reluctant; she didn't see why she should deal with slave traders. She was further insulted when the governor sat on a large throne and she was given a mat on the floor, forcing her to sit below his eye-level. Furious, she made one of her servants kneel on the mat and sat on him! The talks went well, but it wasn't long before the Portuguese went back on their word and the slave traders returned to their old tricks.

In 1626, Mbandi died, Nzingha became King – she refused to let her subjects call her "Queen". When the Portuguese increased their attacks and burned her city, Nzingha retreated to the mountains to regroup. She founded a new kingdom, Matamba, and began a war. For three decades, Nzingha would personally lead battles and guerrilla raids against her old enemy. Her sisters, Mukambu and Kifunji, were her closest advisors, and there were many women in her wider council who also served in the army.

Nzingha offered sanctuary to runaway slaves and Portuguese-trained African soldiers. She sent ambassadors through west and central Africa hoping to create a coalition of African armies. Nzingha found a temporary ally in the Dutch, and the combined forces expelled the Portuguese out of Angola, but it wasn't long before she was forced back into Matamba.

Nzingha changed her approach, now concentrating on building her kingdom as a trading power, though she would still lead her troops into battle when necessary. She died in 1661, at the age of 81, having built a nation who could trade with Europeans on equal terms. She was laid to rest in her leopard skins with her bow over her shoulder and arrows in her hand.

HATSHEPSUT

For centuries, scholars didn't realize that one particular ancient Egyptian king was actually a queen. It may seem strange now, but it was hardly surprising at the time. The few surviving artistic impressions of Hatshepsut showed someone with a man's kilt and body – and a beard. Only in 1822, when hieroglyphics were finally translated, did the truth about Egypt's longest-reigning female pharaoh begin to emerge.

Born around 1507 BCE, Hatshepsut was married to her half-brother Thutmose. Brothers and sisters marrying was common among ancient Egyptian royalty, as they believed it would keep their blood pure.

When Thutmose died, his throne went to Hatshepsut's stepson, also called Thutmose, who was just a baby. Officially queen consort, Hatshepsut was to rule until he was old enough to reign for himself, but she instead declared herself pharaoh, becoming "co-ruler" with the boy. To prove she was as good as a male king, she claimed to be the daughter of a god and had her official portraits depict her as a man with a ceremonial beard and bulging muscles.

Hatshepsut's twenty years as pharaoh were prosperous and mainly peaceable, concentrating on making Egypt flourish. She sent out a spectacular expedition to Punt (possibly modern-day Somalia) that brought back riches, further increasing the country's wealth. She restored buildings and constructed even grander temples and monuments. The greatest of all was the magnificent Temple of Deir el-Bahri at Thebes.

When Hatshepsut died, her stepson, Thutmose III, was finally king. He ruled for another thirty years, building more monuments and proving to be a great warrior. Toward the end of his rule, he tried to erase his stepmother from history, smashing her picture from monuments, destroying records, and building walls around her obelisks. Some people think that Thutmose was angry at having to wait for power, but it's possible he didn't want any challengers to his own son, Amenhotep II.

Hatshepsut's empty sarcophagus was discovered in 1903, but it wasn't until 2007 that her mummy was finally identified. She now lies in the Egyptian Museum in Cairo.

Hatshepsut's stepson tried to erase her from history but fortunately, he failed.

Hatshepsut chose to be painted as a man to portray her strength.

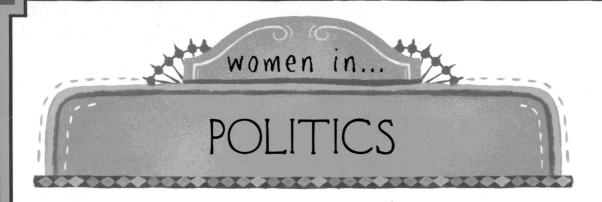

women in...

POLITICS

Until relatively recently, women weren't even allowed to vote. It took several generations of determined women across the world to fight for that right, and some countries have only just permitted women to vote and run for office. Of course that doesn't mean that there were not female political figures before that. Women found – and still find – other ways to make their voices heard. Sometimes the most effective protests are outside government.

Political power is still not equal, but while courageous women continue to make a stand, we creep towards a fairer world.

SIRIMAVO BANDARANAIKE

Sri Lanka

Sirimavo Bandaranaike made history as the world's first female prime minister. She entered politics after her husband was assassinated, and served her country over three terms, always with a strong emphasis on social welfare.

FAITH BANDLER

Australia

Faith's father was kidnapped from the South Sea Islands and taken to Australia as an unpaid labourer. During the 1960s and 70s, Faith fought for the rights of Aboriginal Australians and descendants of South Sea Islanders, demanding – and receiving – recognition as full citizens.

MARTHE GOSTELI

Switzerland

Switzerland only allowed women to vote in 1971. The country uses referendums for constitutional change, and the only people who could vote were men! Marthe could not force men to change, but she was able to persuade them to share power with women.

ANNIE BESANT

UK

In 1888, Annie was shocked by the starvation, wages, and terrible health problems suffered by the female workers at the Bryant & May match factory. She helped organize a strike which led to improvements, and she encouraged others to fight for better working conditions everywhere.

HARRIET TUBMAN

USA

Harriet was born into slavery. After she escaped in 1849, she became a "conductor" on the Underground Railroad, a secret network of safe houses for runaway slaves. She also risked her life working as a spy for the Union Army.

HILLARY CLINTON

USA

Hillary was an active First Lady during her husband Bill's presidency. She went on to serve as a senator for the state of New York and then as Secretary of State under President Barack Obama. She ran for president in 2016 and became the first woman nominated for the ticket by a major party, but ultimately lost the election.

Eleanor was an educated, headstrong royal who fought for what she wanted.

Eleanor bravely went to war with men, but she encouraged chivalry too.

ELEANOR OF AQUITAINE

In the Middle Ages, women were considered to be the property of men. Eleanor of Aquitaine, intelligent, cultured, and strong-minded, thought otherwise. Born sometime around 1122, Eleanor was the eldest daughter of the Duke of Aquitaine. She was given an excellent education, and when her only brother died, fifteen-year-old Eleanor became heir to the Duchy with huge wealth and lands. The king of France was named her guardian, and he immediately announced she would marry his son Louis. Shortly afterward, Louis became king.

In 1147, the Second Crusade began. Armies from all over Europe fought to keep Jerusalem in Christian hands. Louis joined the Crusade and Eleanor promised him a thousand soldiers. Some say she dressed as an Amazon and galloped through the town of Vézelay on a white horse to persuade men to join the cause. She then shocked everyone by saying she was going along too. The crusade was a failure, and Eleanor and her husband returned home on separate ships. Their marriage was annulled in 1152.

Two months later Eleanor travelled to her home state of Poitiers and married Henry of Anjou. He became king of England in 1154, ruling over a vast kingdom. It would be a tempestuous marriage – both king and queen were used to having their own way. Eleanor played an active role in the running of the empire, travelling constantly between France and England. She had five sons and three daughters. She and her husband argued a lot though, and eventually, she moved back to her own lands.

In 1173, she was implicated in a plot by two of her sons against their father. Furious, her husband imprisoned her for the next sixteen years. After Henry's death in 1189, Eleanor's favourite son, Richard I, released her. She acted as regent while Richard (now known as the Lionheart) went to join the Third Crusade, thwarting attempts by her youngest son John to usurp the throne. She helped negotiate Richard's release when he was taken captive, even travelling to Austria to collect him in person.

John came to the throne in 1199. Eleanor was nearly 80 by now, but she crossed the Pyrenees into Spain to fetch her granddaughter Blanche. She later saved John by defending him against her grandson Arthur's rebellion. Eleanor eventually retired to Aquitaine and continued running things there until her death in 1204. Her elegant tomb in the abbey church at Fontevraud shows her reading a book, something very unusual for medieval women.

RANI OF JHANSI

During the nineteenth Century India was part of the British Empire where local rajas (rulers) governed under the British Queen Victoria. Many Indian people hated the foreigners dominating their country, and in 1857 and 1858 resentment boiled into rebellion. Few expected the greatest hero of the Indian Mutiny to turn out to be a heroine.

Born in 1835, "Manikarnika" lost her mother when she was four. She was brought up by her father who worked for the peshwa (ruler) of the princely state of Maratha. Little "Manu" trained in martial arts alongside the boys, learning to shoot, fence, ride horses and elephants, and to read and write, all unusual for a girl at the time. Sadly, her being married off at the age of fourteen was less unusual. Gangadhar Rao was raja of nearby Jhansi and much older than his new rani (queen), renamed Lakshmi Bai, but the two were happy and had a son. Much to their despair, the boy died at four months old. They were devastated. The ageing raja adopted a young boy called Damodar Rao as his heir, before he too, died, it is said, of a broken heart.

The British Governor General, Lord Dalhousie, refused to accept Damodar Rao as the legal heir to the Jhansi throne and declared that the kingdom had "lapsed". Lakshmi Bai's formal appeal on behalf of her adopted son was rejected. An agent of the British East India Company was posted as "protection", the state jewels were confiscated and 22-year-old Lakshmi Bai was told to leave Jhansi Fort. She didn't. In 1857, mutiny broke out throughout India and the British had to turn their attentions to other parts of the empire. Acting as regent for Damodar Rao, Lakshmi Bai reinforced her defences and assembled an army, many of whom were women.

The British began a counteroffensive. They besieged Jhansi Fort and a fierce two-week battle ensued. Lakshmi Bai refused to surrender, even after her troops were overwhelmed and an army sent to rescue her was defeated. She escaped with a small force of palace guards and headed east to muster more rebels. Her troops moved to the fortress of Gwalior, seizing the treasury and the arsenal. Lakshmi Bai, dressed as a man, led her army to confront a British counterattack led by General Hugh Rose. It is said she fought like a tigress but was killed in the battle. Later, General Rose admitted that the rani, "remarkable for her bravery, cleverness, and perseverance" had been "the most dangerous of all the rebel leaders."

The Indian Mutiny failed, but the Rani of Jhansi was a national heroine. When the Indian National Army created its first female unit, it was named after her. The name of Lakshmi Bai echoes across India even today.

Lakshmi led an army that fought for her adopted son's rightful kingdom.

They called Lakshmi the most dangerous rebel leader because she never surrendered.

Emmeline cleverly manipulated the press, drawing the public's attention to her message.

Emmeline was instrumental in the long fight for women's right to vote.

VOTE FOR WOMEN

EMMELINE PANKHURST

The fight for women's suffrage has been one of the toughest of all feminist campaigns. Emmeline Pankhurst was not the first woman to demand votes for women, but her completely uncompromising approach saw a genteel movement of "slightly eccentric" ladies in the United Kingdom turn into a serious challenge to Edwardian society.

Emmeline Goulden was born in 1858 in Manchester, England. Her family had radical views, and she went to her first meeting about women's suffrage when she was just fourteen. Her husband, Richard Pankhurst, was a lawyer and great supporter of women's rights. His death in 1898 was a shock to Emmeline. She threw herself into her work and helped found the Women's Franchise League, which supported votes for all women, not just single women and widows.

Emmeline was frustrated. Her cause was progressing too slowly; no one was taking votes for women seriously. In October 1903, she co-founded the female-only Women's Social and Political Union. Its motto was "Deeds Not Words". These women were determined to do whatever they had to to get the vote; they were done talking about it. In 1905, Emmeline and her daughter Christabel were arrested for causing trouble at a meeting and the penny dropped. Publicity was the answer, and Emmeline would stop at nothing to get it.

She organized noisy demonstrations which rapidly turned to more extreme measures. The authorities started to get uneasy and the women were given the nickname "suffragettes". Suffragettes chained themselves to railings, smashed windows, vandalized public art, and set fires. If they were sent to prison, they went on hunger strikes, which gained even more publicity. When the prison guards violently force-fed them, it was all over the papers.

In 1913, Emmeline's friend Emily Davison threw herself in front of the king's horse at the Epsom Derby. She died from her injuries, and the campaign became even more bitter. Emmeline was arrested for setting an incendiary device and given three years in prison. Christabel took over, though some people, including her sisters, left the movement because it had become too radical.

In 1914, the First World War broke out and everything changed. Emmeline declared a temporary truce and worked for the war effort. After the war, in 1918, the Representation of the People Act gave voting rights to women over 30, and later that year another bill saw women gain the right to stand for Parliament. Emmeline Pankhurst died on 14th June, 1928, just before women were granted completely equal voting rights with men.

SIMONE DE BEAUVOIR

Simone de Beauvoir spoke out about the way women have been treated through history, and once she had raised the subject, it was impossible for the world to ignore it any more.

Simone was born in Paris, France, in 1908. Her mother was a strict Roman Catholic, and she went to a Catholic school. She even considered becoming a nun, but at the age of fourteen she suddenly had a religious crisis and declared herself an atheist. She started thinking about people's place in the world through the individual choices we each make. Today, this idea is called "existentialism".

Simone studied maths, literature, and philosophy and was a star pupil. In 1926, she was accepted into the Sorbonne, one of France's greatest universities. She was top of her philosophy class, where she met another brilliant student, Jean-Paul Sartre. The pair formed an intellectual and romantic partnership that would last the rest of their lives, though they never married, had children, or even lived in the same house.

The Nazi army occupied Paris during the Second World War, and Simone was dismissed from her teaching post. Both she and Jean-Paul would work for the underground French Resistance movement against the Nazis. Unable to teach, Simone started writing. She wrote novels, articles, travel pieces, and memoirs, as well as works of philosophy. She and Jean-Paul founded a journal called *Les Temps Modernes* (*Modern Times*), where she started thinking about the lives of women.

In 1949, she published her most famous work. *Le Deuxième Sexe* (*The Second Sex*) discusses the second-rate status women have been subjected to through history. No one had written about the idea in such clear terms before, and while some people were very excited at what this might mean for women in the future, others felt threatened by what Simone was saying. The Pope put the book on his list of forbidden texts.

Simone had never considered herself a "feminist", but she was suddenly famous as one and used her fame to help causes she felt strongly about. She started a feminist section in *Les Temps Modernes*, supported Algeria and Hungary in their fight for independence, and also supported student protests in France in 1968. During the 1970s, when the feminist movement really began to make headway, Simone gave lectures and wrote essays about women's equality.

Simone de Beauvoir died in 1986. She shares a grave with her lifelong partner Jean-Paul Sartre in Paris's Montparnasse Cemetery.

Simone fought for peace, and condemned the Algerian and Vietnam Wars.

Simone discussed the history of gender inequality in a journal she co-founded.

Viola caused a scandal at the movie theater by taking a whites-only seat.

Viola was dragged out of the cinema, imprisoned, and mistreated at court.

VIOLA DESMOND

Everyone's heard of Rosa Parks, the courageous black woman who refused to give up her bus seat to a white passenger and encouraged a generation to fight injustice, but we've only recently begun to celebrate Viola Desmond, a brave Canadian woman who did a very similar thing.

Viola was born in 1914 in Halifax, Nova Scotia. She trained as a beautician and opened her own salon, Vi's Studio of Beauty Culture. She created her own line of products and started the Desmond School of Beauty Culture. Her business expanded across the province.

Canada did not have the same levels of segregation as some areas of the United States at the time, but it certainly had no-go areas for black people. On 8th November 1946, Viola's car broke down. The repair would take several hours, so she decided to go to the movies. At the Roseland Movie Theatre she requested a ticket for the stalls. She went inside, but was told her ticket was for upstairs. She would have to move. Thinking it was a mistake, she asked to exchange the ticket for one in the main hall, offering to pay the difference. But the cashier said, "I'm sorry but I'm not permitted to sell downstairs tickets to you people".

Realizing the cashier was talking about her skin colour, Viola decided to sit in the main hall anyway. The manager told her that he had the right to refuse admission to any objectionable person. Viola pointed out she hadn't been refused admission – she had a ticket! The police were called, and Viola was dragged out of the cinema, injuring her hip and knee. She was taken to jail and held overnight in a cell. The next day she was charged with attempting to defraud the government by refusing to pay a one-cent amusement tax (the difference between upstairs and downstairs), and a judge fined her $26, even though she had offered to pay.

At no point was the issue of Viola's skin colour raised, although it was obvious that was why she had been arrested. Viola filed a civil suit, saying she had been assaulted, prosecuted maliciously, and falsely imprisoned. The suit never made it to trial, and an application to the Supreme Court of Nova Scotia to have her case put aside was rejected on a technicality.

Decades after Viola's death in 1965, her sister, Wanda Robson, at the age of 73, enrolled on a university course. The tutor, Graham Reynolds, started talking about Viola Desmond, who was then only known by a few scholars. She said "That's my sister!" Wanda and Graham worked together to tell the world about Viola's stand. Badly treated in her lifetime, Viola is now honoured by being featured on the new Canadian $10 bill.

MALALA YOUSAFZAI

There are some men in the world who believe women should not be allowed out of the house, let alone receive an education. One particularly extreme group, called the Taliban, are so scared by the idea of girls going to school that they will resort to shooting them. But with girls like Malala Yousafzai fighting back, the Taliban will never win.

Malala was born in 1997, in Swat, Pakistan. Her father Ziauddin was so passionate about girls' education that he founded a school, but everything changed when the Taliban invaded the area. They banned music and television, and they told women to stay in the house. They weren't even allowed to go shopping. Girls were forbidden to go to school. A hundred schools were blown up.

Eleven-year-old Malala was outraged. She made a speech called, "How dare the Taliban take away my basic right to education?" and started blogging for the BBC's Urdu service about life under Taliban control. Malala continued to go to school and encouraged other girls to join her. In 2011, Malala was nominated for the Children's Peace Prize. The Taliban swore to kill her, but she still went to school. In 2012, Malala and her schoolmates were travelling home when their bus was stopped. Two masked gunmen boarded and shot Malala in the head. Seriously wounded, Malala was put into a medically induced coma so her body wouldn't shut down. She was flown to Birmingham in England, and operated on several times, and luckily, her brain was undamaged.

The Taliban were furious. In trying to silence Malala by shooting her in the head, they had brought more attention to her cause and the protests across the world were even louder than Malala herself had been. Two million people signed a petition for the right to girls' education and the National Assembly quickly passed Pakistan's first Right to Education Bill. The Malala Fund was created to demand a right to at least twelve years of good quality education for everyone.

Malala left the hospital, and by March 2013, was well enough to go to a school in Birmingham. She gave a speech at the United Nations on her sixteenth birthday and wrote a memoir, called I Am Malala, which was also made into a movie. In 2014, she won the Nobel Peace Prize. She donated all the money to build a secondary school for girls in Pakistan. She was appointed a United Nations Messenger of Peace in 2017.

The Taliban still consider Malala Yousafzai a target. Malala takes that in her stride. She says she will not stop campaigning until every child can go to school. Her mother says that's fine as long as she cleans her room first.

Malala won a Nobel Peace Prize and continues to promote girls' education.

Malala was shot for continuing to attend school against the Taliban's wishes.

women in...

SCIENCE

Curious women have sought answers to the universe ever since the ancient Greek mathematician Hypatia. Girls haven't always been encouraged to study science, and they have sometimes been prevented from following their dreams, but many of those who have persisted have made extraordinary, exciting discoveries.

Today there are more women in science than ever before, but there are still fewer female scientists than male. There is a whole universe out there to explore, and amazing, lab-coated women of the past and present show us what can be done when girls are determined to find out the secrets of our world.

MARIE CURIE
Poland

Marie and her husband Pierre studied the invisible rays given off by the substance uranium. They also earned a Nobel Prize in Physics for research on radiation. Marie continued their work even after Pierre died and earned a second Nobel Prize in Chemistry for discovering two new elements, polonium and radium.

ADA LOVELACE
UK

Daughter of the famous poet, Lord Byron, Ada is now better known as a mathematician and writer, and creator of the first algorithm intended to be carried out by a machine, making her the first computer programmer. She is also credited with being the first person to recognise the full potential of a "computing machine".

MAGGIE ADERIN-POCOCK
UK

Maggie has overcome an interrupted education and dyslexia through her love of science and astronomy. She built her own telescope and many scientific instruments, including some for the Gemini Observatory in Chile. She also presents *The Sky at Night*.

HARRIET CHALMERS ADAMS
USA

Harriet explored Central and South America, Europe, Asia, the Philippines, West Indies, and the Gobi Desert via horseback, mule, and on foot in horrific weather conditions. In 1913 she became one of the first women admitted to Britain's Royal Geographical Society.

MARGARET HAMILTON
USA

There were no coding teachers when Margaret started writing software for the Apollo space program. She knew there weren't any second chances if she got her calculations wrong, but her code took humanity to the moon and enabled the astronauts to return safely.

RACHEL CARSON
USA

Rachel was a marine biologist who first warned the world about the dangers of pesticides to the environment. Her ideas made people think about the ecosystem around them and led to a ban on harmful chemicals and the birth of the ecology movement.

Mary discovered entire dinosaur skeletons without receiving proper credit in her lifetime.

Mary braved dangerous, slippery rock faces after storms to find fossils.

MARY ANNING

When Mary Anning was a child, no one knew about dinosaurs. If people dug up gigantic, strange bones, they made up stories about monsters to explain them. Mary didn't train as a scientist and only left her home town once, but her discoveries helped changed science forever.

She was born in 1799 in the English seaside town of Lyme Regis. One of nine children, only Mary and her brother Joseph survived childhood. The family were very poor but her father, a carpenter, used to take the children for walks along the shore to collect shells. They sold the best ones to rich holidaymakers as souvenirs, from a stall on the seafront. Sometimes the "shells" they picked up were very strange indeed. Mary was befriended by a lady named Elizabeth Philpot. Although nearly twenty years older, Elizabeth recognized the young girl's talent and instructed her to read about geology and learn about the fossils she was finding.

In 1811, Joseph spotted a skull sticking out of a rock. He and Mary chipped it out a year later, and Mary returned to the spot after a storm and discovered the rest of the skeleton. She had found the first complete ichthyosaur. Her find was recorded in the *Philosophical Transactions of the Royal Society,* a scientific journal in the UK, but it was not going to be easy for Mary to gain recognition. She was a girl, and she had no scientific education.

Then tragedy struck. Mary's father fell from a cliff and was killed. The family were destitute. They burned furniture to keep warm and were nearly starving. It was dangerous to collect fossils. Her father had died on the rocks and the best time to look for fossils was after a storm when new layers were exposed, but Mary hoisted up the voluminous skirts women had to wear in those days and got collecting. She had some narrow escapes herself.

In 1821, she found a giant sea reptile called a plesiosaur. In 1828, she found *Dimorphodon macronyx*, the first pterosaur discovered outside of Germany and the first complete example found anywhere. Scientists were very excited. They wrote letters and travelled down to Lyme just to meet her, but Mary, never seen without her dog Tray, was still desperately poor. Often, the men who bought her fossils claimed the glory for themselves, and she was only allowed to be an "honorary" member of the Geological Society of London because she was a woman.

Mary Anning was finally awarded a small pension by the British Association for the Advancement of Science in 1838, and on her death in 1847, allowed her the honour of an obituary in the quarterly journal of the Geological Society. The Society continued to ban female members until 1904.

VALENTINA TERESHKOVA

The Space Race between the United States of America and the Union of Soviet Socialist Republics saw two major world powers competing to see who could put the first man on the moon. The USA won that particular race in 1969. In 1963, however, women won a slightly smaller battle when the USSR successfully sent the first woman into space.

Valentina Tereshkova was born in 1937 in a village in Western Russia. Her father was killed during the Second World War, so her mother had to support three children by working in a textile factory. Valentina went to school until she was ten, then started to work in the factory herself. She missed school though, and she continued her education herself through a correspondence course. She also adored parachuting and spent as much of her spare time on her hobby as she could.

The war ended, but the USA and the USSR each wanted to show their citizens they were the most important country in the world through their space programs. Amazing things were happening at a very fast rate. Both countries recruited the best scientists, engineers, and computer experts to build spacecraft, and both countries needed people to fly them. The Americans called their pilots astronauts; the Soviets called theirs cosmonauts.

The Soviets wanted to be first to send a female cosmonaut into space and were very interested in Valentina's experience as a parachutist. She was recruited with three other women, trained, then chosen to fly the spacecraft Vostok 6. Over nearly three days Valentina orbited the earth 48 times, wearing a modified space suit and strapped to the ejector seat. She held Vostok 6 steady using the manual controls and finally fired the rocket that would release the craft out of orbit. There was only one way down: parachuting 6,000 m.

Valentina was given the title Hero of the Soviet Union. She represented the USSR at international events and headed the Soviet Committee for Women for 19 years. She was featured on postage stamps and even has a crater on the moon named after her. Her beloved Vostok 6, "my best and most beautiful friend," travels the world in exhibitions to inspire a new generation. Now in her eighties, Valentina still dreams of flying to Mars, even if it's only a one-way trip.

However honored Valentina was by her country, once the Soviet Union had achieved the record, they were uninterested in repeating the experiment. It would be 19 years before a second female cosmonaut would zoom into space, and the first US astronaut, Sally Ride, would have to wait another year on top of that. To this day, no woman has walked on the moon.

Valentina Tereshkova was the first woman in space and a skilled parachutist.

Even in her eighties, Valentina dreams of continuing to break barriers by visiting Mars.

Rita won a Nobel Prize for her ground-breaking research into nerve growth.

Rita built a lab in her bedroom when Jewish medics were banned.

RITA LEVI-MONTALCINI

It's hard performing ground-breaking experiments that will eventually lead to treatments for diseases such as Alzheimer's and cancer. Now try doing it in a makeshift lab in your bedroom while you're hiding from the Nazis. Rita Levi-Montalcini spent much of the Second World War avoiding Hitler's army and still came up with Nobel Prize-winning science.

Rita was born in Turin, Italy, in 1909. As a young adult, Rita was desperate to study medicine. Her father reluctantly agreed, and Rita earned a degree in medicine and surgery in 1936. She stayed at the university to work, where she developed a technique for staining nerve cells with silver so they could be seen under a microscope. In 1938, the fascist dictator Benito Mussolini decreed that people with Jewish heritage could no longer work in universities or professions, including medicine. Rita's family was Jewish. Unable to work at the university, she built a laboratory in her bedroom, fashioning instruments out of sewing needles and other useful objects she found.

Rita had been intrigued by an article written in 1934 by American embryologist Viktor Hamburger, where he described nerve development in chicken embryos. She used her silver-staining technique to recreate and improve his experiments as the Second World War raged around her. Rita was working as a doctor in a refugee camp when Professor Hamburger saw the papers she'd published about his chicken embryo research. He invited her to visit Washington University in St. Louis in the United States. Rita went to visit Viktor Hamburger for a "short trip" in 1947, and she never left. Her work was so valuable she became a professor herself.

Professor Hamburger showed Rita a mouse tumour that had spurred nerve growth after being grafted onto a chicken embryo. Rita was very excited, and adapted the experiment so the tumour only got a blood supply from the embryo. She repeated the results with nerve tissue, then began working with a biochemist called Stanley Cohen. Together they isolated a protein that stimulates nerve growth in nearby cells. At first people didn't recognize the significance of Rita and Stanley's discovery, but it slowly became clear that it could be used in finding treatments for serious conditions. The pair shared a Nobel Prize in Medicine in 1986, the highest honour of all.

Keen to ensure research continued, Rita founded the Institute of Cell Biology in 1962, an educational foundation in 1992, and the European Brain Research Institute in 2002. She died in 2012 at the age of 103. Even at the end of her life, Rita Levi-Montalcini continued her serious scientific research every day.

CHIEN-SHIUNG WU

Nuclear physicist Chien-Shiung Wu was born in 1912 to an engineer father and a teacher mother. In 1930, Wu enrolled at one of the most prestigious Chinese learning instititutions, Nanjing University, and after hearing about the pioneering work of Polish physicist Marie Curie, it didn't take long for her to switch from studying maths to physics. She graduated top of her class in 1934.

Wu taught for a year at the National Chekiang University in Hangzhou and worked in a physics lab at the Academia Sinica. It was here she conducted her first research in X-ray crystallography. Her female professor, Jing-Wei Gu, encouraged her to continue her studies in the United States, and in 1936 Wu joined the University of California at Berkeley, studying the fission products of uranium. A fellow physics student, Luke Chia-Liu Yuan, suggested she stay and pursue a Ph.D. Wu and Luke would eventually marry, and in 1942, they moved to the east coast where Luke worked at Princeton University. A few years later, Princeton accepted Wu as well. She was the first female instructor ever hired to join the faculty, but she still wasn't a professor.

In 1944, she joined a secret government program that later became famous as the Manhattan Project. Wu developed a process to enrich uranium ore that would eventually be used to create atomic bombs. She also improved Geiger counters for measuring nuclear radiation levels. She left the project in 1945 as the leading expert in her field.

Two of Wu's male colleagues wanted to prove that a particular law of physics didn't work, and asked Wu to devise an experiment that would demonstrate that their calculations were correct. She used cobalt-60, a radioactive form of cobalt metal, to do exactly that. The work resulted in a Nobel Prize – for her male colleagues. Wu once said, "I wonder whether the tiny atoms and nuclei, or the mathematical symbols, or the DNA molecules, have any preference for either masculine or feminine treatment."

Wu never did win a Nobel Prize, though she won many other awards: medals, prizes, and honorary degrees; and was even named Scientist of the Year by *Industrial Research* Magazine. In 1976, she was the first woman to serve as president of the American Physical Society and, perhaps best of all, became the first living scientist to have an asteroid named after her!

Wu finally turned to medicine, studying the causes of the disease sickle-cell anaemia. She retired in 1981, and remembering the prejudice she'd experienced as a female scientist, devoted her time to promoting girls' education around the world. The "First Lady of Physics" died in 1997 at the age of 84.

Chien-Shiung was passionate about the education of young girls.

Wu was an important nuclear-physicist whose discoveries changed physics forever.

NATIONAL MEDAL OF SCIENCE

Elena pioneered female academia as the first woman to receive a Ph.D.

Elena was so religious and charitable that people considered her a saint.

ELENA CORNARO PISCOPIA

Universities have existed for centuries, but they were the domain of men until recently. Elena Cornaro Piscopia, the first woman to ever receive a Ph.D degree, proved female students can learn with the best.

Elena was born in Venice in 1646. When she was seven, the family priest noticed she was very bright and suggested she take lessons in Greek and Latin. She earned the title Oraculum Septilingue, which meant she had mastered seven languages, as well as her own. She also studied mathematics, philosophy, music, grammar, dialectics, and astronomy, but her favourite subject was theology, the study of religion. She wanted to be a nun, but her father wouldn't allow it. He did allow her to go to university, though no one expected her to actually graduate. She was a girl!

By the time she was nineteen, Elena was considered the most learned woman in Italy. In 1672, her philosophy and theology tutors suggested she should work towards a degree at the University of Padua as a doctor of theology. The Bishop of Padua, thinking Elena wanted a degree in philosophy, was shocked when he realized that the degree she was aiming for was in his own discipline. He refused to let Elena study theology, but grumpily allowed her to work towards a degree in philosophy, which included a lot of debating.

Elena was good at debating. Oral examinations, then called "defences", were usually held in the University buildings, but so many people wanted to hear Elena speak that they moved her defence to the cathedral. For the exam, she had to explain, in both Greek and Latin, two passages, chosen at random, from the Greek philosopher Aristotle. She argued eloquently and passionately and became the first-ever woman to receive the traditional laurel wreath, ermine cape, gold ring, and book that showed she was a Doctor of Philosophy. Elena eventually earned all the credits to be awarded a degree in theology, too, but she was never allowed to receive it.

Elena joined the Benedictine religious order as an "oblate" – someone who carries out charitable duties from home. She helped the poor and sick while studying, lecturing, and meeting students from all over Europe. When she died in 1684, the poor people of Padua ran through the streets shouting that a saint had been lost.

Elena paved the way for all women who want to go to university, but it would be a long road. The University of Padua did not award another PhD to a woman for more than 300 years.

MARY JACKSON

When Mary Winston Jackson started her career, female engineers were very rare. Black female engineers were almost unheard of. At the beginning of the Space Age, Mary was probably the only African-American female aeronautical engineer in her field.

Born in 1921 in Hampton, Virginia, Mary graduated from Hampton Institute in 1924 with a dual degree in maths and physical science. There weren't many job opportunities for her though. After a year of teaching mathematics in Maryland, she found herself working as a receptionist, bookkeeper, and secretary before she managed to find anyone to use her skills.

The National Advisory Committee for Aeronautics (NACA) was the predecessor to the more famous National Aeronautics and Space Administration (NASA). Mary spent two years as an aeronautical engineer in the "computing pool" of "human computers". It was a step up from the other jobs, but Virginia State Law still enforced discrimination in the workplace. There were separate toilets marked "White" and "Coloured". White people were allowed to eat in the cafeteria, but black people had to buy their lunch and eat it back at their desks. Mary hated it.

 She aired her complaints with a supervisor, Kazimierz Czarnecki. He was impressed with her brilliance and invited her to work with him – as an engineer. He was experimenting with a supersonic pressure-tunnel, which was capable of blasting models with winds nearly twice the speed of sound. Mary was interested in what happened to the air around those objects. She needed extra qualifications though, and classes, like everything else, were segregated. Mary had to get special permission to join the all-white class, but when she completed the course she finally gained promotion to become NASA's first black female engineer in 1958. She and a handful of other African-American women joined her at a pivotal point in the US space program. For years, she worked hard, but she was frustrated at the lack of promotion, which nearly always went to white men.

In 1979, Mary left engineering. She became the Federal Women's Program Manager at the Office of Equal Opportunity Programs, concentrating on hiring and promoting a whole new generation of female NASA mathematicians, engineers, and scientists. She also worked on many organizations and committees outside work, including the Girl Scouts of America.

Mary retired in 1985. She had won the Apollo Group Achievement Award, done incredibly valuable engineering work, and perhaps most importantly of all, helped other young women to go further than she had been allowed in her own day. She died in February 2005 at the age of 83.

Mary was the very first black female engineer to work at NASA.

Black women had limited opportunities, but Mary worked to improve this injustice.

Nettie worked hard as a teacher to pay for her own education.

Nettie's revolutionary discoveries about how genes work are still used today.

NETTIE STEVENS

What determines whether a baby will be a boy or a girl? For thousands of years nobody knew. There were all kinds of theories. Perhaps it was what the mother ate, or maybe it was whether she was hot or cold. Maybe it was prayer or just plain luck. Nettie Stevens set out to discover the answer.

Nettie was born in 1861 in Vermont, USA. Her carpenter father earned enough money to send his children to school, but not much more. Nettie was a brilliant student and consistently top of the class, but she couldn't afford to go to university. One of the only jobs available to women in those days was teaching, so Nettie would teach for a few months, saving as much as possible, so she could study. When the money ran out, she'd go back to work again. In 1896, Nettie finally saved enough money to go to Stanford University in California. She still spent her summers working at Hopkins Seaside Laboratory, studying the anatomy of microscopic organisms. She gained her degree in biology in 1899.

Nettie continued to Bryn Mawr College in Pennsylvania. For once, she didn't have to worry about cash, as she'd been awarded a fellowship to study abroad. In the labs at the University of Würzburg in Germany, a scientist called Theodor Boveri was investigating chromosomes – little thread-like structures inside cells that carry genetic information. He was trying to work out what role chromosomes had in heredity. Nettie was fascinated.

In 1903, she gained a PhD and started working as an assistant at the Carnegie Institute. Still really interested in sex-determination, she chose to study mealworms as a simple example of all animal life. It was known that offspring inherit equal numbers of chromosomes from their parents, but no one knew what this meant. Nettie discovered that male sperm carries both X- and Y-type chromosomes, while female eggs just carry two X-type. This means the sex of offspring can only be decided by the male sperm. We now call it the XY sex-determination system. Another geneticist, Edmund Wilson, made a similar discovery at the same time, but Nettie's work is considered the biggest leap in ideas. It was the first time someone had proved a connection between a physical characteristic – in this case gender – and chromosomes.

Nettie Stevens's career was brief, but hugely important. The hours Nettie spent staring down microscopes at creepy crawlies lay the foundation for virtually everything we know about genes.

STEPHANIE KWOLEK

You don't have to be a superhero to save thousands of lives. Stephanie Kwolek spent her life in chemistry labs, yet her amazing invention, Kevlar, is so important that it has a fan club!

Stephanie was born in 1923, in Pennsylvania, USA. She loved fabrics, sewing with her mother, and exploring the countryside with her father. When she got older, Stephanie briefly considered being a fashion designer before deciding on a medical career. She didn't have the money to go to medical school, so she went to the Women's College of Carnegie Mellon University instead. She also applied for a temporary research position as a chemist at the DuPont Company. She was interviewed by an inventor called William Hale Charch, who was so impressed that he called his secretary and dictated an offer letter on the spot.

Stephanie loved research so much that she dropped any thoughts of medical school and concentrated on chemistry. She worked on projects trying to create new polymers (chains of molecules that form to make different substances) and ways to make existing processes work at lower temperatures. She also worked on Lycra and Nomex (used in firefighters' gloves).

Stephanie discovered that the molecules of some polymers could be lined up to make extremely long chains, creating strong, stiff fibres. The liquid crystals formed a strange fluid and went milky when stirred. The person in charge of the testing equipment refused to let Stephanie put the goop into his device as he thought it would clog up the tiny holes. When he was finally persuaded to try it, however, it produced a long thread, unlike anything ever seen before. Stephanie was delighted, thinking "Fibre B" might be useful for car tyres.

Now that she had a method, Stephanie and her team were able to make many new fibres. The most famous is Kevlar, which is extremely lightweight, yet five times as strong as steel and resistant to wear, corrosion, and flames. This makes it perfect for bullet-proof vests, but it's also used in safety helmets and protective clothing. Kevlar can be found in aeroplanes, drums, frying pans, mobile phones, skis, and even suspension bridges and has saved untold thousands of lives.

Stephanie eventually received many awards for the technology behind Kevlar and was inducted into the National Inventors Hall of Fame in 1994. In 1996 she received the National Medal of Technology and then in 1997, the Perkin Medal. In 2003 , she was inducted into the National Women's Hall of Fame. Thousands of people saved by Kevlar owe her their lives.

The Kevlar Survivors' Club, founded in 1987 by police officers who owe their lives to the vest, has more than 3,100 members. All of them, and countless thousands more, raise thanks to Stephanie Kwolek.

Stephanie invented a new fibre called Kevlar while working as a researcher.

Protective vests made from Kevlar have saved thousands of lives.

women in...

SPORT

The dedication, training, and effort that goes into being an athlete can be very tough. Long hours, early mornings, and difficult sacrifices all play a part in the race for glory.

Athletes inspire us for all kinds of reasons. Some awe us with their supreme talent and power. Others overcome physical difficulties, difficult backgrounds, poverty, or oppressive political regimes as they battle through to victory. Female athletes often have extra hurdles to clear, such as prejudice, lack of facilities, and in some cases, lack of interest from their own sport. They are not always "winners" in the traditional sense. Some even come last in their races. What we admire is their sheer grit and determination. If they can do it, so can we.

MAGGIE ALFONSI
UK

Maggie was born in London, England to South African parents, with a club foot that she had to overcome to play rugby. She was the first female player in fifty years to win the Pat Marshall Award from the Rugby Union Writers, Club, and was named *Sunday Times* Sportswoman of the Year in 2010.

LAURA DEKKER
Netherlands

The Dutch government said it was unsafe for Laura to sail around the world on her own, but she had properly trained for many years, as all athletes should, and in 2012, she became the youngest person to sail solo around the world at the age of sixteen.

NATALIE DU TOIT
South Africa

Natalie lost her leg in an accident when she was a teenager. Within a few months she was back swimming, even though she could not yet walk. She competed in Paralympic Games and World Cups, and in 2008, she became the first amputee to compete in the able-bodied Olympic Games in more than a century.

STAMATA REVITHI
Greece

Stamata ran the marathon course at the first modern Olympics in 1896 in her petticoat, despite the fact that, as a woman, she'd been banned. She took five and a half hours, but said she'd have done it in three if she hadn't kept stopping to buy oranges!

NADIA COMĂNECI
Romania

At the age of fourteen, Nadia became the first gymnast to be awarded an Olympic "perfect ten". She achieved seven perfect scores and won many gold medals, but training in Eastern Europe in those days was extremely harsh. She defected to the USA in 1981.

JUTTA KLEINSCHMIDT
Germany

Jutta started racing on motorcycles, but in 1995, she began to help develop a new racing car. In 2001, she became the first – and so far only – woman to win the Paris–Dakar Rally, the toughest motor race in the world.

Serena has won an amazing four Olympic gold medals.

She has ventured off the court to promote the welfare of women.

SERENA WILLIAMS

Even if you're born with supreme talent, success is only possible through hard work. Serena Williams always knew what she wanted – to be the best tennis player in the world, and she started young, spending countless hours pursuing her dream and securing her magnificent rise to success.

Born in Michigan, USA, in 1981, Serena started training at three years old, joining her older sister Venus on the courts. Their father Richard was determined to see his daughters succeed and learned how to coach them from books and videos. Venus was a stunning player, but Serena just outdid her. Now living in California, Richard knew that his coaching wasn't serious enough for his daughters' skills, so the family moved again, from Compton to Florida.

Serena turned professional in 1995. Her first Grand Slam win was in 1999, when she beat her sister. The two remain close, even today, however, and pair up to become a daunting doubles team, which won them three olympic gold medals. By 2002 there was no doubt Serena was the number one female tennis player in the world. She had everything: great forehand and backhand, a killer serve, mental supremacy, and a personality that made her a true champion.

Serena has had some health issues, as do all athletes, but she just powers back. Serena's humanity spills into whatever she does. Her joy when she wins is obvious, and her fans experience it with her, something they have lots of opportunities to do. She's won 23 grand slam singles titles, and has at many times been the reigning champion of all four major tournaments at the same time, a feat they call the Serena Slam.

Serena has no trouble standing up for herself, and for others. She tells the crowd if they're being disrespectful, and calls out racist comments and critiques of her body. Off the courts, she has ventured into fashion with her own clothing line and jewellery collection. She also founded the Serena Fund, which helps the victims of violence and promotes education for all. With her sister Venus, she created a fund to build and supply schools in Kenya, Jamaica, and Compton.

Serena Williams is a supreme athlete, perhaps the best the world has known. She is still at the top of her game, even winning the Australian open for a record seventh time, while eight weeks pregnant!

KATHRINE SWITZER

The Boston Marathon has long been a very popular event. In 1966, anyone could enter – as long as they were a man. Kathrine Switzer didn't see why she couldn't join too. She registered, received her race number, 261, and lined up at the start with the other runners. She hadn't run two miles before a race official started shouting at her, demanding she leave the course. When she didn't, he tried to physically drag her off the route and Kathrine's life changed forever.

Kathrine was born in Germany in 1947 to an American family. She trained as a journalist but her true love was running. Her coach told her that women were too fragile to run marathons, which was a common myth at the time. Kathrine was determined to prove everyone wrong. She trained hard and entered the race using her initials, K.V. Switzer, on the entry form. About a mile and a half in, a race official noticed and shouted at her, pulling at her number-bib and trying to drag her off the road and stop her from running the race. Kathrine slipped from his grip and finished the race in four hours, twenty minutes.

Kathrine's first reaction was embarrassment, but her "shame" quickly turned to anger. She wasn't the only angry person; Women everywhere were furious. A photographer had caught the incident, and the resulting image would go on to be one of the most famous photographs ever taken at a sporting event. Kathrine made a decision to devote her life to fighting for the kind of sporting opportunities for girls she had been denied. She teamed up with the cosmetic company Avon to provide these opportunities and reached more than a million women in 27 countries. The Boston Marathon finally allowed women to compete in 1972. Kathrine kept lobbying for a women's marathon at the Olympic Games, and finally succeeded at Los Angeles in 1984.

Kathrine is an Emmy award-winning broadcaster and has worked for many major TV networks covering more than 200 events. She motivates others by writing books and articles and through speaking. She has received many sporting awards, and her place in the National Women's Hall of Fame celebrates both her running and the barriers she broke for women's sport.

Two-Six-One Fearless, the number on Kathrine's original running bib, is a global community that empowers women to discover freedom through running, whatever their ability, body type, religion, ethnicity, or socio-economic status. In 2017, aged seventy, Kathrine Switzer once again crossed the line of the Boston Marathon just 25 minutes slower than her original time, wearing her 261 bib. The number has now been retired in her honour.

Kathrine loved running, but women weren't allowed to run marathons.

Kathrine fought for women to have the same sporting opportunities as men.

Marta has tackled poverty and prejudice to become an inspiring sporting star.

Marta's a superb female footballer, who wants people to appreciate women's football.

MARTA VIEIRA DA SILVA

At home in Brazil she's known as "Pelé con faldas" (Pelé with skirts). To the rest of the world she is just "Marta". Possibly the finest female football player of all time, Marta Vieira da Silva has known prejudice and poverty, yet has risen above it all to inspire young women across the world.

She was born in 1986 in the small town of Dois Riachos. She adored football and joined in as many street games with the local kids as she could. She was often shunned by the boys, however, who hated being beaten by a girl. Her father and her brothers were furious, saying it was unladylike. It was, after all, only seven years after Brazil had lifted the ban on women playing at all.

Too poor to afford a ball of her own, Marta would kick abandoned deflated footballs. It was tough, but she persisted. If she could kick a broken ball straight, she'd be unstoppable with a real one. When she was fourteen, Marta heard that one of Brazil's big clubs, Vasco da Gama, was holding tryouts for a women's team. She took a chance, travelling three days on a sweltering bus. Coach Helena Pacheco was intrigued by the newcomer. Marta's style was rustic, but she was a fast learner. She made the team and was voted best player at her first championship. She was able to send a little money home, but when the women's team at Vasco da Gama was axed, Marta was left without a club. A coach from Sweden saw her and tracked down someone who could speak Portuguese so he could invite her to join Umeå IK. She was seventeen. Sweden takes women's football very seriously and Marta blossomed, leading the team to championship glory three times.

In 2009 Marta signed a contract to play on a team in the women's soccer league in the United States, but due to the league's financial problems, she ended up in Sweden again. She is hailed for her incredible performances but does not earn anywhere near the salary of what even lesser male players receive.

Sadly, there is still much to be achieved in women's football. Marta is an outspoken advocate for girl's football, especially in Brazil, which does not take the women's game seriously. Marta led Brazil at the 2004 and 2008 Olympics and the 2011 World Cup, but when she made a new scoring record of fifteen goals in World Cup play in 2015, her country hardly noticed.

In a country where most soccer teams have a beauty queen but not a female football team, Marta Vieira da Silva, five-time FIFA World Player of the Year, is outraged by suggestions that women wear makeup and short-shorts so that people will watch their games. Everyone, whoever they are and whatever they look like, should be able to play the Beautiful Game.

YANI TSENG

Women golfers go back almost as far as the game itself. Mary, Queen of Scots, was a keen player and is even said to have invented the concept of a "caddie" (assistant). Like all sports, there are a few players that rise above the rest to become something very special. Yani Tseng has been astonishing golf fans since her early teens.

Yani was born in 1989, in Guishan, Taiwan. Her mother was a caddie and her father a top amateur player. Both of them encouraged her from a very early age, and she started playing at six years old. Her first coach, Tony Kao, knew that although Yani needed to practise five hours a day, if she didn't have fun, she'd burn out. He helped her develop her swing speed by encouraging her to hit the ball as hard as she could. Her balls went all over the place, but she was getting fast. She also got really good at hitting balls out of the rough grass! Gradually the balls started going in a straight line and Yani gained confidence. By the age of twelve, she was an accomplished amateur player.

Yani's family moved to California in the United States so she could continue training. Her host, Ernie Huang, also became her mentor. She was one of the top golfers in her age group and in 2002, she won the girls' 13-14 age division at the Callaway Junior World Golf Championships. In 2003, she started working with a new coach, Glen Daugherty. A year later, she won the US Women's Amateur Public Links Championship.

Yani turned professional in 2007 and joined the Ladies' Professional Golf Association tour the following year, when she won the Louise Suggs Rolex Rookie of the Year. She started working with yet another new coach, Gary Gilchrist, who specialized in working with juniors. He worked to improve Yani's swing without actually changing it. It worked. She enjoyed several tournament victories and rose to the top of the women's world rankings. She was winning awards and prizes everywhere she went and became the youngest women's golfer to surpass US $5 million in career earnings (she has currently earned in excess of US $10 million).

There's an LPGA tradition at the Mission Hills Country Club. Anyone who scores a winning putt dives into the lake! Yani dived into Poppie's Pond with a huge smile on her face, even though she couldn't swim. Yani may not have even reached her best yet. Strong, athletic, and highly focused, she remains a formidable and hugely popular golfer, but she still finds time for fun. She enjoys other sports, watching movies, shopping, and hanging out with her friends.

Yani is the youngest female golfer ever to earn over US $5 million.

Yani became the Louise Suggs Rolex Rookie of the Year after turning professional.

Robina competed at the Olympics and paved the way for female Afghan athletes.

1038

Beijing 1001

Robina's presence was symbolic because many Afghans thought women belonged at home.

ROBINA MUQIMYAR

A native of war-torn Kabul, Afghanistan, Robina Muqimyar was not supposed to be an athlete. Living under the oppressive rule of the Taliban, an extreme Islamist group who took power in the 1990s, girls were forced to cover their entire bodies on the rare occasions they were even allowed out of the house, and they were certainly not allowed to play games. The International Olympic Committee punished the Taliban by not allowing any Afghan athletes to compete in the Olympic Games. After the Taliban lost power 2001, Afghanistan was allowed to rejoin the event, as long as women were included. But where were these women athletes to come from?

Robina was born in 1986. Girls were not allowed to go to school, so Robina was educated at home by her parents. She loved to run, but training was impossible during the civil war. She had been told that if she disobeyed orders she would have her nose cut off. The threats were serious. Under the Taliban, the local sports stadium had been used for floggings and executions.

Robina heard that women would be given a spot in the 2004 Athens Games, and she was so excited that she was waiting outside with her application form when the office opened. She and judo contestant Friba Rezayee were chosen, much against the wishes of many traditional community leaders. Robina did not have a stadium to practice in, so she ran in the streets without starting blocks.

While the other runners were wearing high tech shorts and vests, Robina wore long green track pants, T-shirt, and a hijab. She came seventh out of eight runners. Friba didn't win either, but that wasn't the point. Both women had won something far more important than a medal – they had represented the hidden women of Afghanistan at the top sporting competition in the world.

Four years later in 2008, Robina hadn't intended to compete in the Beijing Olympics, but the woman who was going to run defected at the last moment. Robina couldn't bear to think that Afghan women would not be represented, so at the last moment, she ran again. She came last, but the fact that she was there at all was hugely symbolic.

Afghan women are now allowed to train (at different times than the men), but some men still object to women being allowed out of the home. Now known as Robina Jalali, she is on the Afghan National Olympic Committee, working to promote sport for all young people. She even ran for Parliament in 2010. Robina battles on, the true embodiment of the Olympic spirit.

women in...

MUSIC, FILM & TV

Female performers entertained throughout the ancient world, but somehow, over the centuries, women's voices became lost. By William Shakespeare's day they were not even allowed onstage. Boys played all the female roles. As always, a few courageous souls paved a path for the rest of us.

Today, more and more women are making their mark as performers, composers, directors, and producers, and there is someone exciting to inspire in every field of entertainment. Yet there is always room for more! The extraordinary dancer Martha Graham once said that everyone is unique, with something special to give the world. It is up to each of us to make sure the world doesn't miss out on that gift.

SHONDA RHIMES
USA

While watching TV at home with her daughter, Shonda Rhimes decided to try writing a script herself. *Grey's Anatomy* hit the small screen in 2005, making Shonda the first African-American woman to create and executive-produce a top-10 series on network television.

BJÖRK
Iceland

Björk is an award-winning singer, songwriter, actress, DJ, and producer. Throughout her career, she has experimented with many different musical styles, and is famous for mixing them with her unique electronic sound. She is also famous for her unique style, wearing outfits that are works of art.

SELENA QUINTANILLA
USA

The "Queen of Tejano" (Latin American music), Selena's promising career was cut short when she was murdered at the age of 23. She had already inspired a generation of music lovers who had never experienced Latin music before, and she became the first Latin artist to ever debut with a number one album.

LAVERNE COX
USA

Star of *Orange is the New Black*, Laverne Cox is the first high-profile transgender actress. Taunted at school with racist and homophobic jibes, Laverne found strength inside herself to create her own unique space in the world.

ANN HUI
China

Ann Hui is one of Hong Kong's most versatile film directors and actors. From horror to martial arts, comedy to serious drama, she treats each new project on its own merits, rather than imposing her "style". She is in huge demand.

MARGARET HUGHES
UK

Many people believe that when, in 1660, Margaret "Peg" Hughes stepped onto the stage at the Vere Street Theatre to play Desdemona in Shakespeare's *Othello* she became Britain's first professional actress.

Beyoncé began in a girl band but now she's a solo sensation.

Beyoncé dances and sings live, and her performances are legendary.

BEYONCÉ

Beyoncé Knowles is one of the few true superstars who are known by their first name alone. Born in 1981, in Houston, Texas, her talent was evident from an early age. She went to a performing arts school where she started singing with her cousin Kelly Rowland and a couple of classmates. They formed a group called Girl's Tyme. With Beyoncé's dad Mathew as manager, they had a little success and signed with Columbia Records in 1996 under the name Destiny's Child.

Their first album, *Destiny's Child*, eventually sold a million copies, but the second, *The Writing's on the Wall*, sold nine million. Destiny's Child were hugely popular, and after a few line-up changes, Beyoncé and Kelly were joined by Michelle Williams.

Beyoncé started playing with other projects – 2001 saw her acting debut with *Carmen: A Hip Hopera*, followed by the Austin Powers comedy *Goldmember*. Her first solo album, *Dangerously in Love*, was released in 2003 and featured Missy Elliott and rapper Jay-Z. The title of Destiny's Child's last studio album, *Destiny Fulfilled,* in 2004, was prophetic; the group split the following year.

Now completely solo, Beyoncé skyrocketed. Her second album was a massive hit, as was the musical movie *Dreamgirls*. In 2008, she married rapper, Jay-Z in a private ceremony attended by her Destiny's Child bandmates, amongst others.

Beyoncé portrayed beloved blues star Etta James in *Cadillac Records* and she sang James' classic "At Last" at President Barack Obama's inaugural ball. She also began a clothing line called House of Dereon with her mother and launched her own perfume. She was joined by her former bandmates Michelle Williams and Kelly Rowland for an unforgettable halftime show at the Super Bowl in 2013, and her second appearance in February 2016 contained a highly-charged political message that reached millions, something politicians can only dream of.

Beyoncé is the only artist in history whose six studio albums have all topped the Billboard charts. At the 2010 Grammys she was honoured six times. Her fifth album, *Lemonade*, wasn't even pre-announced; it was released exclusively on iTunes and sold more than 800,000 copies on its first weekend.

Beyoncé is an inspiration to women in all walks of life, not least other singers. In Feburary 2017, her *Lemonade* album failed to win Album of the Year at the Grammy Awards. The prize went to Adele, who dedicated hers to her idol: Beyoncé.

ARETHA FRANKLIN

One of the most powerful voices in music, the story of the Queen of Soul has inspired women, singers, African-Americans, and all people for nearly 75 years.

Born in Memphis, Tennessee, in 1942, Aretha taught herself to play the piano as a child and recorded an album, *Songs of Faith*, at the age of 14 at her father's church. In the early 1960s, she signed with Columbia Records and released her first professional album, *Aretha*, before moving to Atlantic Records where, with producer Jerry Wexler, she released a string of hit singles. "Respect" reached number one on the R&B and pop charts and won her two Grammy awards. More hits followed, including "Natural Woman" and "Say a Little Prayer".

Aretha felt passionately about the Black Power movement and fighting for African-American rights during the 1960s. In a period where African-Americans faced many struggles, Aretha's music demanded respect. In 1968, she sang at the funeral of Martin Luther King Jr. and at the Democratic National Convention in Chicago.

Though her career waned in the 1970s, with the disco craze making soul music seem old-fashioned, a cameo performance in the blockbuster movie *The Blues Brothers* helped to revive her career. Her rendition of the song "Think" found her a new generation of fans, and this time they weren't going away.

Though she divorced twice, and her father died during this time, her career was booming. In 1985, she collaborated with the bestselling singer Annie Lennox on "Sisters are Doin' it for Themselves", a song which became an anthem for women everywhere.

Aretha duetted with George Michael and became the first female artist in the Rock and Roll Hall of Fame. She sang at the inauguration of presidents Jimmy Carter and Bill Clinton. In 2003, she founded her own label, Aretha Records, and in 2008, she received her eighteenth Grammy. In the same year, she performed at a third presidential inauguration, but this one was particularly special. It was for Barack Obama, the first black president of the United States.

The Queen of Soul is still at the height of her power. At the age of 74 she announced she was planning to retire after collaborating with Stevie Wonder. Maybe she will.

Aretha is musical royalty and shows no signs of relinquishing her crown.

Aretha has sung for presidents, as well as leaders of the Black Power movement.

Fanny rebelled by publishing her own music, which is now gaining recognition.

Held back by men's traditional views, Fanny's talent was unable to shine.

FANNY MENDELSSOHN

Classical music lovers throughout the world celebrate Felix Mendelssohn, one of the nineteenth century's finest composers. Far fewer people have heard of his sister Fanny, though some people, including Queen Victoria, preferred Fanny's work to her brother's. Yet even today, most of her 466 compositions remain unpublished.

Born in Berlin in 1805, Fanny grew up in a wealthy German family. She and her younger brother Felix received music lessons together. Felix, being a boy, was allowed to travel, become a composer, and meet famous musicians. Fanny, being a girl, was given a talk by her father. The 14-year-old was told she would one day become a wife and mother. It wasn't seemly for young ladies to play music in public or – heaven forbid – publish their own compositions! Stuck at home, Fanny was restricted to *lieder* (songs) and piano pieces that wouldn't upset anyone. She did compose a quartet in 1822, and she quietly published five lieder and a duet under her brother's name, which, of course, meant he got the glory.

Fanny's husband, Wilhelm Hensel, was nothing like her father. Wilhelm encouraged his wife to compose music, play for people, and publish her work. In 1839, the Hensels spent a year travelling in Italy. Fanny finally received some recognition and mixed with musicians and artists who appreciated her work. She loved it. On her return, she completed her most important work, "Das Jahr" ("The Year"), making her the only person of her day to musically interpret the twelve months of the year. She really wanted her work printed, but Felix explicitly objected.

In 1846, Fanny found the courage to defy her brother. She began by publishing some early work, but in 1847, to everyone's horror, she died of a stroke during a rehearsal. Felix may not have wanted his sister to publish, but her death affected him badly. He fell into a deep depression and started printing Fanny's work himself. Just six months later, he too suddenly died.

No more of Fanny's work would be published until the 1970s. Even then the Easter Sonata was attributed to Felix. When the manuscript was tracked down in 2010 and Fanny's handwriting recognized, some people insisted she must have copied it out for her brother! After a lot of detective work, the manuscript was proved to match pages missing from Fanny's music book.

More than 200 years after her birth, Fanny Mendelssohn's talent is finally being acknowledged. There is still much of her music to discover.

LEA SALONGA

The world of musical theatre is fiercely competitive and is constantly finding new stars, but every so often a performer comes along whose talent is so extraordinary that they have no equal. Lea Salonga's powerful voice and perfect pitch have delighted a generation.

Maria Lea Carmen Imutan Salonga was born in 1971 in Manila in the Philippines. She started her career when she was seven, playing one of the children in the musical *The King and I*. She went on to star in several other musicals, and when she was ten she recorded her first album, *Small Voice*, which was given a gold certificate. She also had her own TV variety show, called *Love, Lea*.

In 1989, some producers were having trouble finding a strong enough lead for a new West End musical they were creating, called *Miss Saigon*. It was particularly hard as the music required a very wide singing range, from high to low. Their search for a star took them across the world, but when they heard Lea, they knew they had found the perfect Kim. It was to be Lea's big break. She was a huge hit, repeating her success on Broadway, too. She won a Tony Award and was so popular that when the show finally closed, she was invited back to both London and New York to play the last performances.

Lea's Tony Award was joined by a host of others as she played in hit musical after hit musical. She was the first woman of Asian origin to play Éponine in *Les Misérables* on Broadway and later returned to play Fantine in the same show. She is also the first full-blooded Filipina to win the Olivier, Tony, Drama Desk, Outer Critics' Circle, and Theatre World awards. Lea is perhaps best known for her voicings of two much-loved Disney characters, Princess Jasmine in *Aladdin* and Fa Mulan in *Mulan* and *Mulan II*. In 2011, she was named a Hero of Disney.

Lea made her concert debut in 2005 at Carnegie Hall, and since then has toured the world performing concerts, cabaret, and special events. She has sung for many VIPs, including six Philippine presidents, three American presidents, and Diana, Princess of Wales. In turn, she also listens to other people sing; in 2010, she was one of a panel of judges in an online singing and songwriting contest, and she is currently one of the judges on the Philippines version of The Voice.

In 2010, Lea was appointed as a Goodwill Ambassador by the Food and Agriculture Organization of the United Nations, raising both funds and awareness for various charities fighting poverty, injustice, and hunger across the world.

Even a global superstar needs some downtime. When she's not inspiring the world, Lea Salonga loves to play video games.

Lea helps disadvantaged people through her role as a UN Goodwill Ambassador.

Lea is a multi award-winning actress who voiced Disney's Jasmine and Mulan.

Nora had a talent for turning boring news stories into comedic gold.

Nora wrote and directed Oscar-nominated films, which remain relevant and well-loved today.

NORA EPHRON

Nora Ephron once noted that Hollywood had never been interested in making movies by or about women. To rectify this, she made movies with messages hidden behind romantic plots.

Nora was born in New York City in 1941. Her parents, who were both scriptwriters, turned her rebellious student days into a Hollywood movie. "Everything is copy", her mother would say, meaning that everything in life, however painful or funny, can be used in stories. Nora later used this idea in her own work.

After leaving college in 1962, she started working for *Newsweek* as a "mail girl", however she left when she realized women weren't allowed to write for the paper. Instead, she began writing for a satirical magazine, making fun of another famous newspaper, the *New York Post*. Nora's parodies were so sharp that the paper wisely decided to hire her themselves. She was often given the low-key stories to cover, but she learnt how to write "around a subject", using her own experiences. Her essays were honest, direct, and hilarious.

In 1983, Nora and her friend Alice Arlen wrote the screenplay for a movie called *Silkwood*. The film earned Nora an Oscar nomination for Best Original Screenplay. After this, she made a few more movies that were less successful. Then, in 1989, she worked on *When Harry Met Sally* — a sharp, funny dig at relationships. It was a massive hit, largely due to Nora's way of making people think at the same time as making them laugh. Nora was Oscar-nominated for a second time and then decided something big. In the future, she would direct movies herself.

Sleepless in Seattle, starring Meg Ryan and Tom Hanks, made US $120m at the box office in 1993 and earned Nora yet another Oscar nomination. It's still beloved today. Nora, Meg, and Tom would reunite for *You've Got Mail* in 1998.

Although Nora's romantic comedies seem sweet and unrealistic, they tell us a lot about our world. Her female characters are strong and sparky – not "better" than men, but equal to them.

Nora's next big hit came in 2009 when she wrote and directed *Julie and Julia*, a movie about the famous chef Julia Child and a young blogger trying to recreate her dishes. It earned nearly US $130m. Nora was a prolific blogger herself, though she kept one detail about her life secret. She suffered with myelodysplastic syndrome, a very serious illness.

She passed away in 2012, leaving behind a legacy of films that don't just speak about what it's like to be a woman – they speak about what it's like to be human.

OPRAH WINFREY

A billionaire best known for hosting a talk show, Oprah Winfrey's career is extraordinary.

She was born in Kosciusko, Mississippi, in 1954, to a small farming community. Her early years were very difficult and gave her a sense of injustice as well as a strong desire to help others. Oprah later went to live with her father in Nashville and began working in radio and TV. At nineteen, she was the youngest person and the first African-American to anchor the news at Nashville's WTVF-TV (previously named WLAC-TV).

She moved to Baltimore where she hosted a chat show called *People are Talking*. Oprah's natural manner and warmth with guests made her hugely popular. After eight years she was invited to Chicago to host a morning show, and it was a great success.

In 1985, Steven Spielberg cast Oprah in his next movie, *The Color Purple*. The novel by Alice Walker was close to Oprah's heart, and her performance earned her an Oscar nomination. The musical version of the story went to Broadway and won eleven Tony awards.

The world-famous *Oprah Winfrey Show* was then launched in 1986, regularly attracting audiences of ten million viewers. Eventually, she took over the programme, starting her own production company called Harpo ("Oprah" backwards). In 1994, Oprah vowed to keep her show free of "tabloid topics". At first ratings fell, but then viewers realized that the subjects Oprah chose were interesting without being cruel, and they came back to her. In 1996, the show began a successful book club segment.

Almost at the same time as *Forbes* magazine named Oprah as the richest African-American in the twentieth century, *Business Week* called her the greatest black philanthropist in American history. Her Angel Network has raised more than US $51 million for charity, including girls' education in South Africa and relief for the victims of Hurricane Katrina. She is also an active campaigner, proposing a bill to create a nationwide database of convicted child abusers, as she was abused as a chid.

Oprah is never scared to try something new. She made a mini-series and starred in Toni Morrison's movie *Beloved*. She co-founded Oxygen Media, a TV channel that creates content specially for women. She also launched her own magazine, started her own network, and a self-help project, Oprah's Life Class, which engages ordinary people with experts online. It is impossible to guess what will come next for Oprah, but it is certain to innovate and inspire.

Oprah uses her platform for good, improving child safety and girls' education.

Oprah is multi-talented. She is a well-loved talk-show host, an author, and an Oscar nominee.

Hedy's ideas about communication systems are vital to modern Wi-Fi technology.

Hedy was more interested in scientific advances than Hollywood glamour.

NEWS

HEDY LAMARR

Movie star Hedy Lamarr once said, "Any girl can be glamorous... all you have to do is stand still and look stupid." It would take decades for the world to realize Hedy was, in fact, very intelligent.

In 1914, Hedy was born Hedwig Eva Maria Kiesler in Austria. She was originally interested in science but began acting instead, appearing in her first movie at sixteen. She starred in a film called *Ecstasy* where she shocked audiences by appearing naked. Armaments millionaire Fritz Mandl noticed her, and he persuaded Hedy to marry him. Jealous and controlling, he forbade her to act, instead making her entertain his dictator friends Adolf Hitler and Benito Mussolini, who were buying weapons from him. Hedy was horrified and ran back to Hollywood.

Hedy's next movie, *Algiers*, sent fan magazines crazy. The readers loved her frank admissions that she wasn't good at dieting and liked burgers, but Hollywood tried to make her into a mysterious glamour-puss. Hedy hated the image of her that they were trying to paint. During her Hollywood career, she starred opposite the leading actors of the day, but she never seemed to find the right movie to reach success. Her last major film, *Samson & Delilah*, was in 1939, then she mostly slipped into the shadows, until the world discovered something very curious about her.

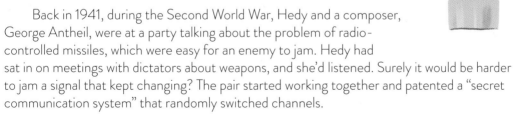

Back in 1941, during the Second World War, Hedy and a composer, George Antheil, were at a party talking about the problem of radio-controlled missiles, which were easy for an enemy to jam. Hedy had sat in on meetings with dictators about weapons, and she'd listened. Surely it would be harder to jam a signal that kept changing? The pair started working together and patented a "secret communication system" that randomly switched channels.

It was a great idea, but the technology of the time wasn't capable of putting "frequency hopping" into action. Besides, an actress had thought it up, which annoyed some people in the military. However, today, "spread spectrum technology" plays a crucial role in GPS, Wi-fi, Bluetooth, and even mobile phones. When Hedy was eventually informed that her idea was brilliant, she replied, "It's about time."

Hedy Lamarr passed away in 2000, having received several prestigious awards. The Austrian prize for inventing and a Harvard University achievement award both bear her name, and European Inventors' Day falls on her birthday. Take that, Hollywood!

GURINDER CHADHA

The characters of Gurinder Chadha and the worlds they live in have a remarkable way of speaking to everyone who watches them. Full of enthusiasm, she knows how to get the best from people around her.

Born in Kenya in 1960, Gurinder's parents moved to London when she was a baby. She grew up in Southall, an area with a very vibrant and diverse culture, where her parents owned a shop. Her life was not privileged, but she was always curious about other cultures and was fascinated by her own mixed cultural identity. She started working in radio and TV before setting up her own production company, Umbi Films.

Gurinder made her first film, a documentary called *I'm British But...*, in 1989, followed by her first feature film, *Bhaji on the Beach*, which followed a group of Asian women on a day trip to Blackpool. *Bhaji on the Beach* brought her wide recognition, and she won a BAFTA for it. Her work presented a fusion of Indian and British cultures in a way that had never been seen before, and it was a hit with critics and the public alike. She moved to Los Angeles to make her next feature, *What's Cooking?*, where she explored four families of diverse backgrounds preparing for Thanksgiving. For Gurinder, diversity always triumphs over difference, and food is a fantastic insight into the way cultures work.

Her most famous film to date is *Bend it Like Beckham*. The story of a young Asian woman from Southall who wants to be a footballer, the movie

was full of humour and charm, and British Asians and people from other cultures all found something in the film that spoke to them. She continued to blend British and Asian traditions with *Bride and Prejudice*, a Bollywood update of a Jane Austen classic, and hit box office gold with the comedy *Angus, Thongs and Perfect Snogging*.

Gurinder was awarded an OBE in 2006, and was delighted to receive an award that she believes represents Britain's past, both good and bad, because she sees herself as a product of that past, and a part of modern Britain. With so many cultural backgrounds, Gurinder has chosen to embrace them all.

Gurinder enjoys capturing diverse communities on film.

Gurinder's talent and unique take on British life led to her gaining an OBE.

women in...

LITERATURE

Women's voices can only be heard properly if they are recorded. In the past, girl's education wasn't considered important. The few women who could read and write tended to be wealthy. From ancient Greek poet Sappho to modern times, however, despite their lack of opportunities women have always managed to create superb literature.

Today, female writers stand shoulder to shoulder with their male counterparts and regularly win top prizes. Hilary Mantel recently won a second Man Booker Prize for her *Wolf Hall* series, and Frances Hardinge's *The Lie Tree*, aimed at young people, beat every other category, including adult fiction, to win the coveted Costa Book Award.

AGATHA CHRISTIE
UK

Author of 66 detective novels, 14 short stories and the world's longest-running play *The Mousetrap*, Christie is the best-selling novelist of all time. She wrote her stories by making endless lists in notebooks, devising complete plots before she even put pen to paper.

CHRISTINE DE PIZAN
Italy

As a professional writer, Christine was very unusual for medieval times. Her 1405 work, *The Book of the City of Ladies*, describes famous historical women as equal to men, something few had ever dared suggest before.

HILDEGARD VON BINGEN
Germany

In 1106, when she was eight, Hildegarde was shut away in a hilltop monastery in Rhineland to be a nun. This didn't stop her creativity. She wrote 9 books, 77 songs and poems, and more than 400 letters. Her exquisite music is still played today.

ALICE WALKER
USA

Alice was accidentally blinded in one eye as a child. Her mother gave her a typewriter, which opened a whole new world. Her novels, stories, and poetry explore the experience of African American women and her most famous work, *The Color Purple*, won the 1983 Pulitzer Prize.

DOROTHY PARKER
USA

Famous for her wisecracks, Dorothy's vicious wit was perfect for super-stylish 1920s Manhattan. Her personal life was not easy, but her sharp, funny reviews, poetry, short stories, and articles for *The New Yorker* magazine were unrivalled.

SEI SHŌNAGON
Japan

The Pillow Book is the closest tenth century Japan got to a blog. Shōnagon was just fourteen when she joined the royal court, and her journal gives us a wonderful record of life there. She's rude about her enemies, romantic about nature and even makes quirky "top-ten"-style lists.

Chimamanda is a prize-winning author whose empowering work helps people understand feminism.

Chimamanda's speeches are inspiring, and she's especially important to young black women.

CHIMAMANDA NGOZI ADICHIE

Not many people see their essay become a set-text for high school students. Even fewer have their TEDx talk sampled by Beyoncé. Chimamanda Ngozi Adichie's work touches a nerve with young people, especially young black women today.

She was born in 1977, in Enugu, Southeastern Nigeria. The fifth of six children, Chimamanda grew up in the house formerly occupied by famous Nigerian writer Chinua Achebe. Her father was Nigeria's first professor of statistics and later became deputy vice chancellor of the University of Nigeria. Her mother also worked at the university, as the first female registrar. Chimamanda went to the university, where she was a bright student and won several prizes. She loved writing and edited her student magazine *Compass* while she was studying medicine and pharmacy.

When she was nineteen, Chimamanda left Nigeria for America, where she won a scholarship to study communication at Drexel University in Philadelphia. She followed it with another degree from Eastern Connecticut State University. She wrote articles for that student magazine, *Campus Lantern*, and was particularly interested in creative writing, and she studied for a master's degree at Johns Hopkins University in Baltimore. In her senior year, she started working on her first novel.

Purple Hibiscus was published in 2003 and was widely acclaimed. Her second novel, *Half of a Yellow Sun*, did even better, and was made into a movie. The story is set before and during the Nigerian Civil War, which is also known as the Biafran War. Chimamanda managed to break through the conflict's politics to focus on the human stories of ordinary Nigerians who were touched by it. Her 2013 novel, *Americanah*, explores what it's like to be black in America today, and is also slated for the silver screen.

In 2012, Chimamanda gave a TEDx talk called "We Should All be Feminists". It's warm-hearted, honest, and entertaining, yet it delivers a powerful message about inequality between men and women in the twenty-first Century. Chimamanda describes issues in Nigeria and Africa, but her words ring true across the world. It was such a huge hit that she adapted it into an essay, which still hits the bestseller lists, and in Sweden it was distributed to every 16-year-old high school student. It was even sampled by Beyoncé in her song *Flawless* and Dior's Spring 2017 collection had, as its central piece, a T-shirt with We Should All Be Feminists written across the front. Thanks, in part at least, to Chimamanda Ngozi Adichie, twenty-first-century feminism is becoming a subject to talk about.

J. K. ROWLING

Before Harry Potter, many adults didn't read children's books, but thanks to Joanne Rowling, children's literature has become cool.

Joanne was born in 1965 in Gloucestershire, England. She had a difficult childhood and her mother was diagnosed with multiple sclerosis, which made life harder. Books and writing became her escape, and she wrote her first story about a rabbit at six years old. While at university, she studied French and classics, which would be very useful later when she was inventing spells, as many of them are based on Latin words.

She had the idea for Harry Potter while sitting on a delayed train to King's Cross, London, in 1990. Joanne used up lots of scraps of paper as she made notes about the plot. She arrived in Edinburgh in 1993, out of work, but with three chapters in her suitcase. She famously wrote in cafés around the city with her baby, Jessica, beside her.

Her first three chapters were rejected by eleven publishers, but the twelfth asked to see the rest of the novel – and accepted it! She was advised to use gender-neutral initials instead of her name because some people thought boys might be put off by books written by a woman. Many years later, when she published a book for adults, she actively chose a male name, Robert Galbraith, for different reasons – she wanted the book to be judged on its merits, not on her fame.

Harry Potter and the Philosopher's Stone, published in 1997, was an almost-instant bestseller. The successive books and films gained even more fans. The series has been translated into 78 languages and sold over 450 million books. People loved it because it wasn't just about magic; it reflected real people and real things. For example, Joanne has been very public about suffering from clinical depression, which she channelled into her dark magical beings, the Dementors.

J. K. Rowling continues to innovate. In 2012, she launched Pottermore, a new digital, way to engage fans. In 2016, the film, *Fantastic Beasts and Where to Find Them* and a two-part play, *Harry Potter and the Cursed Child*, continued the world of Harry Potter further.

Every year Joanne gives much of her money to charity. She has never forgotten what it's like to be poor and knows the importance of generosity and having a dream. After all, who wouldn't want to go to a magical boarding school, cast spells on our teachers, and have an owl as a pet?

Joanne is incredibly charitable and never forgot her own difficult past.

Joanne used initials instead of her full name to avoid gender prejudice.

Tove's first book was published when she was just thirteen years old.

Tove Jansson's writing was relatable because it put common feelings into words.

TOVE JANSSON

Finnish writer and illustrator Tove Jansson's art shows how hope can shine in the darkest hours. Her life shows how a loving family can nurture talent and bring out the best in people.

Tove was born in 1914 in Helsinki. Her father, Viktor, was a sculptor, and her mother, Signe, was a graphic artist. The Jansson house was full of parties and laughter and art. Little Tove could draw almost before she could walk. At night, she would sometimes creep into the pantry, looking for nibbles, and one of her uncles teased her that the "moomintrolls" would catch her.

In 1918, Viktor went to fight in the Finnish Civil War. He returned sad and depressed. The only thing that could cheer him up was a storm, something Tove herself learned to love.

Tove's first book, *Sara and Pelle and the Octopuses of the Water Sprite*, was published when she was 13 years old. No one was surprised when she became an artist, making fine art and illustrations and showing her wicked sense of humour through caricatures for the satirical magazine *Garm*.

She started doodling moomin-type creatures in 1935. They hadn't yet formed into the cuddly characters we love today – in fact they were quite scary. There were, however, scarier things happening in the real world. In 1939, Europe descended into war. Tove was, like so many, extremely distressed. She needed an escape. She sat down and began to write "Once upon a time..." meaning to create a fairy story. She chose her angriest creature and called him the Moomintroll.

The Moomins and the Great Flood was published in 1945. It showed lost creatures searching for loved ones, eventually finding their way to happiness in Moominvalley. In reality, lost people were searching for loved ones across Europe. The terrible natural disaster in her second book, Comet in Moominland, reflects Tove's horror at the dropping of the atomic bombs in Japan in 1945. Tove's fantasy world, with its terrifying sea storms, mountains and caves was balanced with flowers and forests and joy. It allowed children everywhere the chance to hope.

When *Finn Family Moomintroll* was published in English in 1950, it caused a sensation. The Moomins were given a comic strip in the London paper *The Evening News*, reaching over 20 million readers every day. TV animations, plays and even an opera followed.

Tove Jansson died in 2001. She used to say she wrote for "Miffles" – people who felt like outsiders, anxious, and lonely. Perhaps she realized we all feel that way sometimes.

MAYA ANGELOU

In her darkest moments, Maya Angelou found solace in other people's books, music, and poetry. Today, millions find inspiration in hers.

Marguerite Johnson was born in 1928 in St. Louis, Missouri. When her parents divorced, she was sent with her brother Bailey to live with her grandmother in Stamps, Arkansas. Stamps was racially segregated, and Marguerite, nicknamed "Maya", experienced prejudice first hand.

She was taken back into her mother's care, but at the age of seven, she was molested. She told her brother, who then told her family. The man who had attacked her was then found dead. Maya became convinced her voice had killed him, and she lost the power of speech for five years.

Maya started reading early. She would lose herself in stories and poetry, pretending that she was in them herself. One day, a woman invited Maya to her house. Mrs Flowers was kind to her and served her tea, and read to her, helping her to find her voice again.

Maya won a scholarship to study dance and drama. At sixteen-years-old, she became San Francisco's first African-American street car operator. She also gave birth to a son, Guy, and in 1952 married a Greek sailor, despite the prejudice about mixed-race marriages in those days.

She studied dance and became a singer, appearing in the musical *Porgy and Bess*. Never one to settle down, Maya next moved to Africa. She became a newspaper editor, first in Cairo, then in Ghana.

Ever since her time in Stamps, Arkansas, Maya had felt strongly about racial discrimination. In 1964 she returned to the States to help her friend Malcolm X build a civil rights organization. To her horror, Malcolm was assassinated in 1965. She was devastated when another friend, Martin Luther King Jr., was also murdered in 1968.

In the late 1950s, Maya joined the Harlem Writers Guild, supported by the writer James Baldwin. Her memoir *I Know Why the Caged Bird Sings*, published in 1970, was a sensation. She would write 36 books in total, as well as plays, and screenplays. As an actress, she earned a Tony award for *Look Away* and an Emmy for *Roots*.

President Bill Clinton asked Maya to compose a poem for his inauguration in 1993. "On the Pulse of the Morning" is one of her most famous works. Another president, Barack Obama, wrote a great description of Maya: "A brilliant writer, a fierce friend, and a phenomenal woman".

Maya repeatedly witnessed racial injustice and then became involved in fighting it.

Maya is a famous poet who also won Emmy and Tony awards.

Mary's ideas about gender equality made her one of the first feminists.

Mary spoke out passionately against sexism and published articles in radical magazines.

MARY WOLLSTONECRAFT

Mary Wollstonecraft lived in an age we now call the Enlightenment, when the place of men in the world was fiercely debated. Mary wanted to know why women weren't included.

She was born in 1759, in London, England. Her childhood was difficult: her father was abusive and her mother openly favoured her older brother. At nineteen, Mary decided to make her own way in life, but she hated her work as a lady's companion. Mary, her sister Eliza, and her best friend Fanny founded a school instead. Watching her pupils, Mary began to realize she wasn't just resentful of her own family, she was angry at an entire society that was unjust and unequal.

Fanny died in 1785, and Mary was devastated. After, she went to Ireland to work as a governess, but she detested her employer, Lady Kingsborough. Mary saw her pretending to be weak and dependent on men, yet acting manipulatively and cruelly. Disgusted, Mary returned to London where she became a contributor to a magazine called the *Analytical Review*, a radical text founded by Joseph Johnson.

A Vindication of the Rights of Woman is Mary's most famous work. She wrote it in 1792 because she was angry when an otherwise enlightened man, Jean-Jacques Rousseau, said a girl's education should make her useful to and supportive of men. Some had already called for better education for girls, but Mary was demanding something new – equality.

Mary travelled to Paris to observe the French Revolution, and fell for an American named Gilbert Imlay. They had a daughter together, who she named Fanny, but the relationship with Imlay didn't last. Mary eventually returned to London and began spending time with a radical group of people that used to meet at her friend Joseph's home. The group included Thomas Paine, who had written *The Rights of Man*, William Blake, the artist and poet, and William Wordsworth, the poet. There was another man there too, William Godwin. He had free-thinking views similar to Mary's own.

William and Mary didn't believe in marriage, but they did marry when Mary became pregnant again. In 1797, she gave birth to their daughter Mary, who would go on to write the beloved classic *Frankenstein*. Tragically, Mary Wollstonecraft died ten days after she gave birth. William published some of her unfinished work, but it didn't have an immediate effect. Early biographers were outraged by her lifestyle and ignored the serious issues she raised. Mary Wollstonecraft's work was, however, appreciated over time. Today she is celebrated as one of the earliest feminists.

GABRIELA MISTRAL

Lucila Godoy Alcayaga, better known as Gabriela Mistral, captured the pain of being human in a way everyone could relate to. Her exquisite poetry, which centres around loss, the downtrodden, childhood, and maternal love, captivated a nation.

She was born in 1889 in the small town of Vicuña, Chile. Her father was charming and artistic, but he abandoned the family when Lucila was three. She was brought up by her mother, who she adored, and her older sister. While she was still in primary school, Lucila was wrongly accused of stealing school materials, giving her a strong sense of injustice. Lucila loved to write and had work printed in the local paper, including an article in 1906 calling for equal education for girls.

When her mother's health started to fail, Lucila had to leave school and earn money. She became a teaching assistant but wanted to be a proper teacher. The articles she had written about schooling for girls worked against her. She was denied a place at school, in case she caused trouble. Instead, she studied on her own and was always angry that she had been denied education.

When she was seventeen, Lucila fell in love with a man named Romelio Ureta, but he was very troubled and committed suicide. His death changed her forever. Devastated, she threw herself into teaching, wrote more articles about the importance of education for everyone, and published a lot of poems. She would continue to teach both elementary and secondary school for many years until her poetry made her famous enough to write.

Lucila first came to be noticed in 1914 with *Sonetos de la Muerte* (*The Sonnets of Death*). The work won first prize – a gold coin and a flower – in the national competition Juegos Florales. Now known as "Gabriela Mistral", Lucila was famous throughout Latin America.

Gabriela never married or had children, which saddened her, yet her poetry and strong humanitarian views were seeing success. She was awarded the title "Teacher of the Nation" in 1923, taught Spanish Literature in the United States, worked in the cultural committees of the League of Nations, and became the Chilean consul in Italy, Spain, Portugal, France, and the USA.

In 1945, Gabriela was the first Latin American person to be awarded the Nobel Prize for Literature. Right up until her death in 1957, she was passionate about the rights of children, women and the poor. She was concerned about the future of Latin America and continuously strove towards peace.

Gabriela won a Nobel Prize for Literature, despite her limited education.

Gabriela's passions included humanitarianism, social equality, and encouraging young poets to write.

women in...

BUSINESS

Business is yet another world traditionally dominated by men. When women have gone into business, often because they had to, they have proved they can be just as innovative and commercially minded. Many turn out to be better. Sometimes, because they have not been able to follow the "usual" routes, women have found different and exciting ways to bring their products and skills to the marketplace. They have become experts at using imagination in place of capital investment and persuasion instead of brute force, but there is still some way to go in the world of business.

ELIZABETH TAYLOR
UK and USA

Although remembered as a highly celebrated actress, Elizabeth Taylor earned much of her fortune through business endeavours and merchandise, including a perfume called "Passion".

ELIZABETH MALLET
UK

In 1702, Elizabeth Mallet published *The Daily Courant*, the first British daily newspaper. From her London premises, she printed only facts, adding no comment, as she believed people had enough sense to think for themselves.

JOY MANGANO
USA

Single mother Joy invested her life savings in her invention, the Miracle Mop, but she was disappointed when the shopping channel QVC didn't sell many. She promoted the product on TV herself and her honest, enthusiastic approach sent sales skyrocketing. She has since come up with numerous other inventions and has ammassed a huge business empire.

LAURA ASHLEY
UK

While working as a secretary, Laura started designing small items to sell from home. The business she started with her husband Bernard blossomed from small factories, to stores across England, then Europe. She refused an OBE however, because Bernard wasn't offered one too.

JEANNE LANVIN
France

Jeanne opened a hat shop in 1889. She started making clothes for her daughter which were so popular that she opened a young ladies and women's clothes department. Soon a top couturier, Jeanne invented the idea of fashion "season collections".

INDRA NOOYI
India

Indra has worked with some of the world's biggest companies, including Johnson & Johnson, Motorola, and General Electric. She Joined PepsiCo in 1994 and became president and chief executive officer in 2007.

Madam Walker employed hundreds of African-American women, saving them from poverty.

Madam Walker's hair remedies turned her into the first female self-made millionaire.

MADAM C. J. WALKER

In the early years of the twentieth century, women generally did not go into business. Madam C. J. Walker proved that a good idea, hard work, and clever sales techniques could make businesswomen just as successful as their male counterparts. She didn't wait for someone to give her a chance: "I got a start by giving myself a start", she once said.

Sarah Breedlove was born in 1867 on a cotton plantation in the state of Louisiana, in the USA. She was the fifth child of ex-slaves – her parents had just been freed after the American Civil War. Sarah was the first free-born child in the family. Sadly, her parents died when she was seven, so she was sent to live with her sister and brother-in-law in Mississippi, where she picked cotton and also did domestic work. Her brother-in-law mistreated her and the work was hard. When she was fourteen, she married Moses McWilliams, a decent man. They had a daughter, but Moses died when little A'Lelia was two.

Sarah moved to St. Louis to work as a washerwoman, earning $1.50 a day. She married again, to advertising man, Charles J. Walker, but life was still tough. Stress, poor living conditions, and nutrition led to Sarah developing a scalp ailment. It was a common problem, but there was very little available to treat it. She experimented with what was available and invented her own remedies. In 1905, Sarah started selling hair products by Annie Turnbo Malone, a successful entrepreneur, but she soon became convinced she could do better.

The family moved to Denver, Colorado, where, as "Madam C. J. Walker", Sarah traveled between towns giving lectures and demonstrations of The Walker System of Hair Culture, which involved special brushing techniques, heated combs, and her own recipe "Wonderful Hair Grower" shampoos and ointments. By 1908, she had opened a factory and beauty school. Being a "Walker Agent" was a way out of poverty for hundreds of African-American women. Sarah organized clubs and conventions for her representatives, recognizing successful sales, charity, and education.

The first woman ever to become a self-made millionaire, Madam Walker immersed herself in Harlem life. She donated large sums of money to charity, something she had done even when she was only earning pennies. She was especially devoted to the National Association for the Advancement of Coloured People, which would later support Viola Desmond's civil rights case. In 1919, her $5,000 donation to the NAACP's anti-lynching fund was the largest individual donation ever received at the time. Madam C. J. Walker died in 1919, the sole owner of a business valued at more than $1 million. Her personal fortune was between $600,000 and $700,000.

SHERYL SANDBERG

An amazing woman of the twenty-first century, Sheryl Sandberg is chief operating officer of Facebook, proving that women are at the front of the digital revolution. Sheryl was born in 1969 in Washington D.C.. She studied economics at Harvard and graduated with the highest possible honors. Sheryl was especially interested in the way that domestic abuse can lead to economic inequality. She founded a group called Women in Economics and Government because she felt more women should be involved in these subjects.

The same year Sheryl graduated, her former advisor, Lawrence Summers, had become chief economist at the World Bank. He was very impressed with his former student and asked her to join the team as a research assistant. She worked for two years on projects that helped developing countries. She then went to Harvard Business School, where she also earned her MBA. By this time, Lawrence Summers was working as deputy treasury minister for President Bill Clinton. He needed a chief of staff, so Sheryl worked for the president until the next administration arrived.

In 2001, Sheryl become one of the Google's vice presidents. She developed projects including AdWords, and AdSense, and she worked on Google's philanthropy arm, which looks at public health, poverty, and climate change. She is particularly interested in the environment; her house has solar panels and a living roof. Sheryl left Google, and since 2008 she has been chief operating officer at Facebook.

Sheryl is passionate about women building confidence in the workplace. She has noticed that although feminism has achieved a lot, most of the top business executives in the world are still men. She feels women should be more assertive in putting themselves forward, taking the lead without worrying about being thought bossy. She detests even the word "bossy", saying it damages women's confidence. She works towards her goal of empowering women in many ways. Her TED talk, "Why We Have too Few Women Leaders", has been viewed more than seven million times. She helped create a set of photographs to be used in magazines and leaflets that showed working women who didn't look like stereotypes, such as older women and working mums who weren't wearing trouser suits.

Sheryl's book *Lean In* discusses the anxieties women feel about making a place for themselves in the world of work. She encourages them to join small "Lean In circles" and encourage each other to aim for the top. There is still work to do, but Sheryl Sandberg is determined to close what she calls the "Ambition Gap".

Sheryl has had a successful, varied career and has worked for huge technology companies.

Sheryl encourages women to be ambitious and have confidence in the workplace.

Anita worked hard to turn her life experiences into a successful beauty business.

Anita valued environmentalism, social change, body-positivity, and charity work over making money.

ANITA RODDICK

Many businesswomen have used their wealth to help others. Anita Roddick went a step further, turning her entire business into a force for change. The daughter of immigrants, Anita was born in Littlehampton, England, in 1942. She opened the first branch of The Body Shop in Brighton in 1976, having painted the walls dark green to hide the damp. She'd had no training, but her travel and time living abroad on a kibbutz (a community that lives and works together) taught her a lot about how the world worked.

When Anita first opened The Body Shop, she didn't have enough money to bottle all her products. She remembered her mother recycling containers during the war and liked the idea. Europe was just waking up to the idea of environmentalism, and customers approved of the way that The Body Shop used natural, ethically sourced products in reusable bottles. The store was a big success, and soon Anita was able to open another.

Now something of a celebrity, Anita wanted to use her business to promote environmental and social change. She used her influence to highlight problems faced by poor people in developing countries as multinational companies devastated their lands drilling for oil or mass-producing commodities. She joined campaigning groups such as Greenpeace, Amnesty International, and Reprieve, fighting global warming, domestic violence, and other injustices. She collected four million signatures against animal testing for cosmetics, and The Body Shop was one of the first businesses to prohibit the sale of products tested on animals.

Anita wasn't just fighting against things; she wanted to find solutions. She set up a "green pharmacy", creating products using rainforest plants, farmed fairly by local people. She invested in a wind farm. She challenged traditional ideas of what "beauty" looks like by using a UK size-16 doll called Ruby in advertisements. In 1989, she created The Body Shop Foundation, which has since donated more than £24 million to charities and campaigns.

In 2006, Anita sold her business to concentrate on global social issues. She continued working tirelessly, but she died in 2007. True to her life, Dame Anita Roddick left her entire £51 million fortune to charity.

MARGARET HARDENBROECK PHILIPSE

Women's rights come and go, but the very toughest can weather most storms. Margaret Hardenbroeck weathered every storm, on both sea and land, to become one of the most successful merchants in colonial America.

Margaret was born sometime around the middle of the seventeenth century. She moved from Elberfeld in Germany to the Dutch colony of New Amsterdam (later known as New York) where she worked as an agent for her cousin. She arranged for the sale of pins, cooking oil, and vinegar in exchange for American fur.

In 1659, Margaret married a wealthy merchant, Pieter Rudolphus de Vries. She continued trading under her maiden name. When Pieter died in 1661, Margaret didn't miss a beat and took over his business. His business pursuits had been complicated, and Margaret found herself involved in lawsuits. When she was sued, she countersued, and then sued other people. She took no nonsense.

In 1662, she married Frederick Philipse, a former carpenter, under a "usus" licence, which preserved her legal identity and meant she could conduct business herself. The couple signed a prenuptial contract, allowing Margaret to keep various possessions.

Frederick and Margaret became very wealthy. They owned at least four ships, purchased vast amounts of property, and expanded the business. Margaret made frequent trips to Europe as "supercargo", responsible for the purchase and sale of goods. While on board, Margaret was in charge – and everybody knew it. Described as having "unblushing avarice" and "excessive covetousness", she once insisted that everyone on board search for a mop that had fallen overboard.

In 1664, New Amsterdam became a possession of Britain. British laws regarding women were harsh. Margaret was made "feme covert" – she was completely subsumed by her husband and all profits became his property. Despite this, Frederick seemingly didn't take advantage of this and Margaret continued working until she retired around the year 1680.

Margaret was a tough businesswoman, who always took charge in her endeavours.

Margaret travelled the Atlantic by ship, making trade deals and transporting goods.

EPILOGUE

None of the amazing women in this book had an easy life. They've all had to make sacrifices to follow their dreams and achieve such inspirational feats. The many remarkable men through history have had to work hard for their own impressive achievements, but it is important to remember that women have traditionally had an extra layer of prejudice placed upon them.

Through unequal treatment, they have suffered in many seen and unseen ways. Women of colour have experienced this at an even deeper level. Intimidated by strong women, a lot of men have dismissed female power as unnatural, freakish – and, unfortunately, even somewhat "unhinged" at times.

Today, we owe a huge debt of gratitude to the brave women of the world who have dared to make a stand. Thanks to them, women are closer to finding equality with their male counterparts. In most countries, women can vote, run for political office, and can at least apply for jobs that are seen as traditionally male.

Yet there is still a long way to go. The number of top female business executives, scientists, and engineers is nowhere near equal to the number of men in these positions, even though numbers are growing. Some female receptionists are still required to wear high heels and makeup to work. They do so because they have to, rather than because they simply enjoy the style and wish to dress this way. Many women face abuse for the way they look, and then suffer again for calling out their abusers.

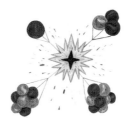
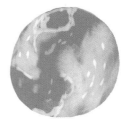

Today, women are legally discriminated against less, yet they still face social prejudice. Social media trolls hound people who don't conform to traditional ideals of beauty. They are too fat, too thin, too old, too young, too ugly, and even "too beautiful". Magazines show "hideous" photos of celebrities in swimsuits with "imperfect" bodies. Many women have extra issues to contend with, such as their skin colour, economic situation, gender identity, or sexual orientation, and in some countries around the world the discrimination they face is unimaginable.

The women in this book blazed a trail to clear the way for us to go further than they were able to so we can blaze one for those who come after us. The best way we can honour them is for each of us to take the opportunities we are given and to create opportunities that don't yet exist. We must take part, do the best we possibly can and continue the fight against inequality. So let's get going – that first woman on the moon slot is still vacant!

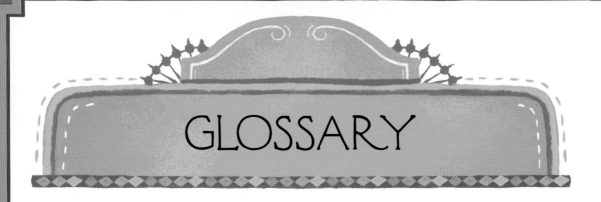

GLOSSARY

Abolitionist – someone who fought for the end of slavery

Aboriginal – a person who is native to Australia

Abstract – something that exists as a thought or idea, without physical evidence

Advocate – a person who fights or campaigns for a specific cause

Aeronautics – the science of flight

Anxiety – a mental state where you feel very worried or nervous

Armaments – military weapons and equipment

Besiege – to attack with an army

Biochemistry – the science of the chemicals within living things

Bust – a sculpture of a person's head and shoulders

Circumnavigate – to travel all the way around the world

Commodity – a raw material that can be bought and sold

Corruption – dishonesty by those in power

Counteroffensive – violence in response to being attacked

Crystallography – the science of crystals

Cubism – a form of art from the early twentieth century, using simple shapes and colours

Depression – a mental illness where a person feels very sad, tired, and hopeless

Dialectics – a form of philosophy where people answer questions by discussing their different opinions

Destitute – very poor

Dictatorship – a government where one person has all the power

Diplomacy – the act of managing the relationships between two or more countries or groups

Discrimination – when someone is treated differently because of their skin colour, gender, sexual orientation, or another reason

Dynasty – a line of people in power who are all from the same family

Dyslexia – a disability where a person finds it difficult to read and write

Ecology – the science of living things and the environment where they live

Economic – to do with money

Embodiment – the physical form of something

Embryo – a living thing, not fully formed yet

Empower – to inspire a person or group of people, giving them the confidence to do something

Entrepreneur – a person who sets up a business

Ethical – something that is morally good

Fission – splitting something into two or more parts

Fusion – mixing two or more things together to create one thing

Homophobia – when someone is treated badly due to their sexual orientation

Humanitarian – concerned with other people's well-being

Incendiary – something that causes fire

Innovative – to do something in a new way

Lieder – a German piece of music for a singer and a piano

Memoir – a book written by a person about a specific part of their own life

Modernism – a form of art that is different from traditional techniques

Mutiny – a rebellion against the people in charge

Native – a person or group of people who are originally from a specific area

Obituary – a piece of writing about someone who has recently died

Observatory – a place where people study the stars

Philanthropy – working towards the wellbeing of others, often by giving a lot of money to charity

Pioneer – a person who does something before anyone else

Pivotal – an important moment that changes how things happen from then on

Predecessor – the person who had a job before the current person in that role

Prophetic – something that predicts the future

Prosperous – very successful, making a lot of money

Radiation – high-energy particles that come from certain elements

Realism – art that shows things as they are, even if it is not pretty or nice

Representative – someone who speaks for a group of people, or a thing that is used as an example of its species, type, or group

Segregation – keeping people separate, often due to their skin colour

Sickle-cell anemia – an illness where blood cells lack the correct nutrients, and become misshapen. This is most common among people of African descent

Specimen – something that is used as an example of its species, group, or type

Suffrage – the right to vote

Surrealism – a form of art that is weird and dream-like

Symbolism – showing or creating a powerful image that represents an idea

Tempestuous – with passionate, but often conflicting, emotions

Transgender – a person whose gender identity is different from the physical body they were born in

Truce – a temporary peace

Unprecedented – something that has never happened before

Uranium – a powerful chemical used in nuclear bombs

Versatile – something with lots of uses

Voluminous – big, with lots of material

CREDITS

Weldon Owen would like to thank the following people for their work on this book:

Nicole Patterson, Thomas McBrien, Susie Rae, Claire Philip, Tayabah Kahn, Bethan Roberts and Katherine Murrant.

We would also like to thank each and every one of the amazing women in this book for their hard work, sacrifices, and courage in the face of adversity and discrimination.

Written by Sandra Lawrence

Sandra Lawrence is an author and journalist from London. Sandra has written for all the broadsheets and regularly contributes features to the *Daily Telegraph* and *Sunday Telegraph*. She has also written for magazines, including *Marie Claire* and *Country Life*.

Illustrated by Nathan Collins

Nathan is an illustrator currently working from a little studio deep in the Welsh valleys. He can often be found sketching away on the hillsides – the natural surroundings inspire him on a daily basis. He loves the rawness of traditional mediums, using them in a combination with digital media to create his work. Nathan acquired his degree in illustration in 2015 from University of Wales Trinity Saint David, and has worked freelance ever since.